Becoming Gutsy & Formidable

Becoming Gutsy & Formidable

ONE LIFE OUT LOUD

Sharyn Holmes

Ⓚ THE KIND PRESS

Trade Paperback ISBN: 978-0-6450113-1-9
eBook ISBN: 978-0-6450113-0-2

Author photo: Ryan Holmes Photography

Print information available on the last page.

The kind press acknowledges Australia's First Nations peoples as the traditional owners and custodians of this country, and we pay our respects to their elders, past and present.

THE
KIND
PRESS

www.thekindpress.com

For Sahra,
through your eyes,
you taught me how to live.

Acknowledgement of Country

I wrote this book on Turrbal, Jagera and Wangerriburra lands. I pay my respects to the Elders past and present and the Traditional Owners of this land. Sovereignty was never ceded. This was, is, and always will be Aboriginal land.

Content Warning

Contained within some chapters of this book are personal stories that might trigger trauma and memories in those who have survived physical and sexual assault. I invite you to read at your discretion. I have added content warnings in each chapter where necessary.

Contents

Introduction

I was once a girl just like you or someone you know. Perhaps a sister, a daughter, a niece, a cousin, a neighbour, a friend. I loved to make things. I'd craft bracelets from red wool and ring pulls from my dad's aluminium beer cans. We'd take the cans down to the local car park for recycling on a Saturday, and this would be my pocket money. At the height of recycling, the cans earned me $1.30 per kilo. I'd spend it on 1980s music swap cards, chewing on the disgusting, unpalatable pink chewing gum that came with each pack. The ones I remember most clearly featured Bryan Ferry and Human League. Other times, my earnings went to magazines with pull-out posters of bands and singers and sweets like toffee apples, coconut rough, Milkos, and Wonder cones (a type of ice cream). In grade 2, the tuckshop lady nicknamed me Wonder Woman after I ate two 50-cent Wonder cones one hot summer's day.

I spent weekends reading books from the moment I woke up. I was an early reader and devoted booklover who sought to escape into another reality, fairy tale or fantasy.

I loved dot-to-dot, colouring-in, making mud pies and playing in the park near the block of flats I lived in until I was nine. I loved to see how high I could go on the swings back when the surface beneath was gravel and the swing structure was huge and made of logs, thick chains and rubber seats.

I'd try and fail at roller skating on the paths around our block of flats in my red and blue size 2 skates before I rapidly outgrew them. I had wished to be a skater girl.

I'd draw, paint, scribble and write stories on the plain and dot matrix paper Dad would bring home for me.

I played with my beautiful Beauty, a smart black and white border collie cross kelpie that Dad brought home one early morning to surprise me when I was in grade 4. We were inseparable and she was my best friend until early adulthood. I still miss her.

On TV I'd watch *Paddington Bear*, *The Wombles*, *The Wind In The Willows*, *The Goodies*, *Catweazle*, *Worzel Gummidge* and *Doctor Who*, and later, *Press Gang*, *Beverly Hills 90210* and *Degrassi High*. Whatever I chose to enjoy, I immersed myself in it, and trying to get me out was quite a feat.

I won books from Encyclopaedia Britannica after entering their spelling competitions.

With a penchant for TV show theme songs and commercial jingles, I'd sing them repeatedly, driving my dad mad like any kid would. Theme songs peppered my 80s life—anthems from *The Muppets* to *Fraggle Rock* and *The Golden Girls*. I listened to 1960s British music from my dad's record collection, the occasional Gene Pitney, Roy Orbison, ABBA, Boney M, Australian Crawl and Billy Idol before entering the 90s during a period of grunge and metal. Soon, however, the 80s came calling again, and I plunged into the deep, the goth, new romantic, electronica, and the industrial music and club scene in early adulthood.

The dancefloor was my church. On the dancefloor, I was free. Under the cover of the strobe lights and smoke machine, I could just be *me*. I could express my emotions, channelling them into dance moves as I heard and felt every beat. I was liberated and energised by this expression. I danced the way I felt and as if no one was watching. Dancing was a 'me' thing, not something I did for anyone else. An introvert dancing for myself, alone. Music moved me. It expressed emotions I didn't have words for. As a young person, I was able to emote, escape or face reality, feel something or block something or dance to soothe my soul on Friday and Saturday nights (and sometimes

Thursdays and Sundays, too). Music soothed my soul, and the poetry of it all helped me understand myself and plumb the depths of my complex sensitivity and the intensity of my emotions and personality. For decades, music has been this for me, and recently, that's evolved and expanded beyond that which I have ever known.

Music is woven into the tapestry of this book. It's my story, with a soundtrack. At the end of this book, you'll find 'The Soundtrack', a list of my favourite music from start to finish. The aim of these songs is to provide a soundtrack to the stories I've shared and to uplift, resonate, deepen, connect and provide words and music that may help you to stretch, dance, heal and grow. The Reflection Questions in each chapter aim to expand your becoming. Take what you need and leave the rest. I hope that through my love for music, words and storytelling, you discover, deepen and broaden your horizons, dreamscapes and healing with beats and rhythms that sing to your heart. May this pathway of reclaiming rhythm in every sense of the word call you to spring forward, take action and question why you would ever deny yourself a gutsier, formidable you.

I was a girl with big dreams once. A girl who harboured a secret dream to be a writer and an author. A girl who was very shy and sensitive but so full of joy, creativity, expression, wonder and oh, so many questions! A few things crossed my path in life which sought to shake me up and dim my light and, on a few of those occasions, I let myself be taken over by their shadow. One day in my early teens the girl I was changed forever; my ascension was temporarily put on hold. I lost her, and I fought every day from that moment to finally reclaim her.

adrienne maree brown (they choose to write their name in all lower case) wrote a blog post about being forty-two years old and what feels true. This line hit me right in the heart: 'Writing is both my life's work and my spiritual practice'. For me too, nothing could be truer. I write so much, thousands of words written in the pages of journals from adolescence and scrawled into the background layers of twenty-seven discarded paintings and numerous art journals never to be read by anyone but me, if ever again.

When I began writing the concept for a book in 2017, I knew I had a lot to say. I also knew I had a lot of learning to do—and fast. It's like I knew that the years ahead would require a rapid integration of these learnings, not by choice, but because life was an oracle in itself and I was getting a heads-up on my prophecy—a preview, if you will. Only thing is, I'm not supernatural. I wish. I kept getting these hints in dreams and altered states beckoning me to seek greater depth. Unsure of the 'how' and without always knowing why, I moved forward to explore and experiment. With one life to live out loud, how was I going to do that knowing there was always a price for speaking out? It was a matter of how much to say and not censoring myself to please others, while still implementing greater boundaries to handle what came my way with grit.

Gutsy life vision

My vision for the gutsy life and person I am growing into has never been clearer. I can't ever recall being this excited about the unknown that lies ahead. I am not worried about it. I am not anxious about it. I can taste the freedom that the unknown brings. I know what anxiety feels like. I know and understand that pain. I survived with dormant, unresolved trauma for twenty-two years.

What I've learned during these years of self-discovery and spirituality is that I have the power to change my life. I do not have to accept the crap. I get to choose how I feel. I can have the cherry on top, not just the crumbs. I can still love myself first and give to others without selling myself short. It's okay to honour the beginnings and the evolution.

For me, dance has always equated to freedom and personal expression. While dance is a healing art form, you don't have to be a 'dancer' to enjoy the benefits. During recent leadership training with my students, the brilliant Lauren White spoke of embodiment and that if a woman was feeling disconnected from her body, one, some or all of the four pillars of embodiment were missing.

I'm going to offer one of these pillars to you now: movement.

Moving your body brings you into a state of presence and awareness of your body. Many of us have suffered shame, judgement and comparison when it comes to our bodies, so we don't take care of them, we look outside for our worth, we tune out and away from our inner knowing and this leads to the fractured relationship we have with ourselves.

I want to remind you that you are so worthy of love and that your body is an essential part of the equation. Your gorgeous body carries you through life and you need it. Show it some love today. It can be as simple as applying body oil or lotion and offering loving thoughts and gratitude to yourself.

Purpose

I believe my story has a purpose, which is why you are holding this book in your hands as I share them with you. I'm telling some of my stories to you. Necessary stories. Painful stories. The experiences I couldn't have done without and others I wish I had a choice about. This is my world and I'm here to share, not escape to another reality as I often did in books and fictional tales in my youth and adult daydreams. This book is about feeling something. Feeling all the feelings that we can feel as humans. Embracing the entire deep-feeling and sensating being that I have always been or am learning to be now that the shades are lifting.

I have learned that accepting anything at face value is far away from the depths I want to plumb in this life. We only live a life of survival alone if we go through the motions on autopilot, numb and not facing what we are able to do: feel. I'm not here to just survive and scrape by (I've already had my fill of that), I'm here to thrive, and it took me far too long to realise that I was living a half-life. I suppressed my being-ness. I repressed the belief that I was worthy of anything good. I felt undesirable and ugly. I didn't fit the mould. Maybe I am here to break it? I fell madly in love anyway and I still was living a half-life. I became a mother, and I was still numb and felt broken on the inside. I wasn't enjoying life as much as I could have. I knew it. There was no denying it. Just awareness, some shame and notions of 'what the fuck am I going to do about it?' because it was, and is, down to me.

The reality for me is that dormant, unhealed and active trauma affected my whole person. Today, I feel I'm in the very early days of *accepting* my whole person. Behold, the midlife self-acceptance in progress here. It feels pretty raw and fresh. I continue to process and give some insights along the way.

Have you noticed that life revelations have a habit of striking hard and all at once? It's said 'when it rains, it pours'. I live in a subtropical city that floods so that phrase is quite literal here.

When you read this book, there are personal stories mere months old and personal stories decades old. I knew somehow that I was whole, but I didn't *feel* whole. I felt like I had been treading water my entire life, and how I sustained it for so long, I do not know. A weak swimmer in the pool or ocean, paddling frantically between spaces and places, looking elsewhere instead of placing the spotlight on myself. It was now or never. Sink or swim. The clock went on ticking, and doing things differently couldn't be delayed any longer.

There's this exchange in the TV show *Buffy the Vampire Slayer*, where Sarah Michelle Gellar's character Buffy says to her ex-boyfriend Angel (David Boreanaz), 'Okay. I'm cookie dough... I'm not done baking. I'm not finished becoming whoever the hell it is I'm gonna turn out to be. I make it through this, and the next thing, and the next thing, and maybe one day, I turn around and realize I'm ready. I'm cookies. And then, you know, if I want someone to eat m- or enjoy warm, delicious, cookie me, then... that's fine. That'll be then... when I'm done.'

Becoming Gutsy and Formidable is my 'I'm becoming cookies' story. A story of the journey to becoming gutsy and how I saved myself through art, creativity, motherhood, jewellery making, leadership, activism, remembering my true essence, owning my power and my voice and using it for humankind. This is a story of taking hold of the wheel of my life and living with feeling, conviction and becoming formidable. It is also a story of one human collecting all the pieces of their soul along the way and coming to freshly realise and embrace a neurodivergent life of lessons, stories and memories with self-acceptance at the heart of it—all at age forty-five.

Unabridged living is possible. Sometimes we have to take a long road to journey back to our heart's home. It's okay to be the tortoise. I wish I had remembered that when I got lost. Life is more of a rollercoaster than a fairy tale, at least in my experience. From the journey I've taken so far and the road ahead, this is what I know: you are the rescuer you seek. You will be the one to defend your realm. You are the one on the horse with the flowing mane. You are the one who will be victorious in your pursuit of purpose, passion and living your potential. Take a closer look at what you learn about yourself from the lightbulb moments. If you are going to be fierce in who you are and the paths you will take, then fierce devotion is key, because you are one hundred percent worthy to resist every obstacle, ceiling and roadblock that dares to cross your path. You, too, are becoming gutsy and formidable.

Stories with a soundtrack

At the end of this book, there is a list—'The Soundtrack'—of recommended tunes so you can purchase and listen to the song that embodies and emotes the personal stories I share. I will explain more later in the book, but this will help you to travel with me through words, to sensate more deeply and, as you'll soon learn, I am all about depth. I welcome you to this tome, my story, and what I hope will aid your becoming. Let's get this adventure started. Here are a few tunes for you to kickstart our ride together.

'Superstar', Seeker Lover Keeper
'The Becoming', Nine Inch Nails
'Pure Morning', Placebo
'Walls', Kings of Leon
'Respect', Aretha Franklin
'Cloudbusting', Kate Bush
'Drive', Incubus
'The Real Thing', Faith No More
'More', The Sisters of Mercy
'Hurricane', Halsey

An ode to you, dear reader

Fiercely disrupting by being you
over cups of tea and coffee,
while focusing on your dreams and
building a magnificent life on your terms.
You don't have to change who you are or become someone else.
You don't have to be louder to play bigger.
You just need to know that you have all that you need inside of you
and that when you harness and trust in those gifts,
you will be the full expression of yourself, nobody else.
You don't have to make videos to be heard.
Those who are for you will find you
no matter what (or so I'm told).
You don't have to be pitch-perfect, airbrushed to perfection, studio lit
or bleached and balayaged to be brilliant.
You are you, and you are golden entirely.
You may move beyond your comfort zone and feel at odds with the
world, but you will know or come to believe that you belong and fully
deserve to be seen, heard and held for the unique gifts that you alone
can bring.
I see you.
I believe in you.
I know you.
I understand you.

Perhaps you crave to 'belong'.

Perhaps you are like me and aren't really sure if you want to. I do love a rebel.

Keep looking.

Keep going.

Please don't stop.

You are needed.

Perhaps you have been scarred by your childhood, relationships and professional life and are at a crossroads, not really sure of your next move.

Me too.

Me too.

Me too.

Everything beyond us is unknown.

We don't have to be afraid. If you are, that's okay.

We don't have to know all the answers.

We don't have to feel whole to be whole.

We are already.

Perhaps we need a little more baking to be done.

To feel that we have brought all of our gifts to the table.

For we surely deserve a place at the fucking table. Or the ability to create one of our own.

For thousands of years, our ancestors fought for that right and we are still surviving and up in here fighting.

Our participation is crucial. It's time we said 'yes' to ourselves, whether we feel underprepared to take the stage or not.

Our mission, our passion and our purpose must be fulfilled.

Our generation and the generation of today's children are what's at stake and we are ready to answer the call.

Gaia has heard our call and she is familiar with our roar.

Our way, it's our time and we are ready to truly shine.

1
Belonging

'I dreamed about a culture of belonging. I still dream that dream.
I contemplate what our lives would be like if we knew how to
cultivate awareness, to live mindfully, peacefully; if we learned
habits of being that would bring us closer together, that would
help us build beloved community.'
—bell hooks, Belonging: A Culture of Place

Roots

I was raised to treat people with respect, kindness and generosity. I
learned that these weren't always values taught or followed by others.
To not stare or hurt people. I was raised to form my own opinions
and beliefs, not just the ones taught to me. I was taught to question,
debate and take a stand when it mattered. I was raised by loving and
affectionate parents who worked hard.

My dad was the first person to teach me that I was equal and not less
than or less worthy than someone white. I came home from primary
school one day, I can't recall how old I was at the time, and I was upset
and asked him if I was half-caste, because it seemed like a bad thing
if someone was willing to call me it. I remember him comforting me,
aghast and in defence against what had been said to me, and said,

'Don't you ever say that or feel that way.'

There have been many times since then as I got older when I have forgotten to seek his wise counsel. In recent years, when I remembered that he was always in my corner, I've sought him out and we've talked about lots of different things, from storytelling to mental health. The way my dad has stood up for me while growing up and now as an adult, I can clearly see where my sense of loyalty comes from.

During my teen years and young adulthood, my dad and I had many heated arguments. We would often not speak to each other until the next day, that's how long we needed to cool down our respective fiery tempers. With each argument, I learned it is important to stand for something. To have an opinion even if someone disagrees. My dad never told me to think his way or try to convince me. Though I tried the latter with him a few times in those teenage years! In our minds, we were both right and sometimes we'd take on another viewpoint we hadn't considered. I had the freedom to think and while the air was thick after one of our debates, I learned to never back down if I believed strongly in something. Through this, I can see how I learned how to feel in my gut and slowly I developed the instinct to trust it. There never was a 'Dad knows better' scenario. When we talked in this way, we were equals, individual people with a point of view. I've had similar arguments and debates with other people and the glaring difference is that they would always tell me I was wrong, call me names, read into what I was saying as though they knew my mind better than I did, insult me, tell me how I should feel (even if they knew far less about the topic or had no experience), shut me down, try to get me to agree with them—which was never going to happen—or walk away when I wouldn't.

My dad taught me respect and conviction in our dialogues together. I enjoy heated debates, however, I am still learning and seeking people who can take the heat and stay in the room.

Trinities

I notice things that come in threes. My first trinity: Ma, Dad and me. My second: Depeche Mode, Nine Inch Nails and The Cure. My third: my husband, Ryan, my daughter, Sahra and me.

It may be seen to be blasphemous to use the Holy Trinity as my template phrasing, but here we are.

My parents provided me with a solid foundation in life, one grounded in kindness, love, connection, generosity and a strong work ethic.

Over the years I have had moments where I took my beginnings for granted. In full appreciation of my roots and what has been able to grow from them, I say this: family isn't always perfect, but mine helped me to grow myself freely, accepting me the way I am (without knowing just how a big deal that is to me now, thank you, Ma and Dad), supporting and encouraging me, and providing me a lifetime of wonderful memories, happiness and laughter that has called me back to myself time and again when I lose myself. I may not have had faith in myself, but Ma and Dad always did. They watched the extended, years-long, phase where I wore black PVC, crushed velvet and lace clothing every weekend to the goth nightclubs I frequented with my friends. We've exchanged a fair few odd glances because of my textural yet noir expression, but not once did my parents ask me to re-think my outfit or try to change me. I was free to be me. They instilled that in me. The tongue piercing (disposed of seven years ago) and multiple tattoos were a little more questionable, but accepted, nonetheless. All of me was.

My second trinity offered me euphoria and elevation. Numerous hours on the dancefloor dancing the way I feel. Those younger years, while tough when it came to relationships and friendships, had a full body outlet to unleash every weekend to diffuse tension, stress and overthinking. You, on this day, a solo dance party is only a button away.

Music has been a big part of my life from the early days through to now. I analysed it in musicology in years 11 and 12, speaking on The Cure's cover of Jimi Hendrix's 'Purple Haze'. I do love a great cover. Such as Depeche Mode's cover of David Bowie's 'Heroes' and Placebo's cover of Kate Bush's 'Running Up That Hill'. I sought meaning and moods in music. I curated a playlist of my life with songs that brought me back through time and space. Music helped me understand, accept and express my emotive and sensitive nature. Song lyrics were poetry and put into words what I felt when I couldn't find the words myself. They also assisted with my writing process; a word, a beat and a sound could provoke an unleashing of writing.

My third trinity, who has been with me for nearly twenty years, has shown me what love can be, how joyful togetherness is and has provided much laughter and toilet humour. My husband has been a constant source of love and support through all my challenges. My daughter has taught me by her very existence how important it is to strive for and thrive under the knowledge that I, and my beloved family, are stronger together.

Journal entry, 9 April 2016: Good heart

I grew up with my ma telling me how important it is to have a good heart. She still repeats this message to me, and I wholeheartedly believe it to be true. It's something I've tried to embody and practise. Having a good heart is my ma's way of saying be kind, compassionate and generous. I was certainly raised to be all those things and more. My ma showed me how. To this day my automatic response when meeting new people is kindness, compassion and generosity. You could say that I'm an idealist most of the time and yes, sometimes being kind, compassionate and generous has not been valued by the receiver.

Somewhere along the way as we transition from child to teenager to adult, we forget that being kind, compassionate and generous isn't just reserved for others; it is also a gift we need to deliver to ourselves. Life can be pretty stressful, and when we are on autopilot taking care of everyone else's needs we tend to be the first person we overlook. We think harsh thoughts of ourselves, riddling our hearts and minds with criticism, belittling, self-deprecating comments and self-doubt at a time when we need the most compassion.

Journal entry, 24 November 2022: Create where you belong

I made a note some months back to flesh out what it means to 'create where you belong'. My friend Lauren White, who is a confidante, said it at a luxe gathering event she organised late 2021. I will get to what I was thinking at the time and how I was embodying it through the body of work I've created. I've since ruminated on it, and this is what has come up for me now.

Creating where I belong looks like unpacking this house, creating a nice office space and nook for myself, making the daily bed and lounge nests with my various textured blankets, cushions and throws, and laying about in my wine-coloured velour pants and continuing my spell bottle canvas painting project. Since 2020 and the pandemic took hold, we've all spent unimaginable periods of time at home. With a limited social life that barely changed since before the pandemic, I grounded more in home life. Now I realise the enormous effort and energy it takes for me to go out and socialise compared to years ago, and I need more downtime after as well.

At the onset of the pandemic and work-from-home arrangements, my husband was going to be spending seven days a week at home. He may have taken it the wrong way at first because I was content in my working-at-home situation and him being there made it noisier and more distracting. I finally got over myself after a few weeks as we turned our attention to the art of cocktail-making at home and trying various gins. This was followed sometime later by my purchase of an air fryer which I had wanted for about five years.

Finally, after the gloss of DIY gin cocktails wore off, I was back in the kitchen with my various vegetables and spices to experiment and test out in the air fryer. That air fryer got quite a workout in those first couple of weeks at our house as I perfected how I cooked my chips. I started to get my love of cooking back again, but it was slow going as I was bored and overwhelmed about shopping, meal planning and preparation decisions. It was one of many increasing signs that something had been going on with me for a long time, I just hadn't landed on what that was yet.

At Lauren's prompting, I realised that everything I was creating in my coaching business and body of work from 2018 onwards was to create belonging and togetherness for others. I wanted to spend more time with likeminded people and with the pandemic bursting the bubble on in-person events, virtual events and spaces were what I focused on creating (I write about it in 'Chapter 14: Formidable Voices'). I realised it wasn't possible to create something where I didn't belong. It was innate to me to feel a part of not only the act of creation but the active space-holding of the work and writing I created. It was the recognition of that active space-holding over the past four years that I realised I had been holding for others far more than I had for myself. I wasn't in any groups where I was held, and that depletion was growing in size and awareness and couldn't be ignored.

Today, creating where I belong is about home and nourishment more than it is about creating more work and spaces, mainly because I know my energetic capacity and I've felt spent for many months now. I require a period of time to refuel before I do what I once did again or regroup to decide how I might change it in future to be sustainable and healthy for me and beneficial all-round. These considerations are so necessary when we are deep and sensitive feelers and/or neurodivergent and caregivers, too. We need time, space, safety and nourishment to function, perhaps more than other people, and that's okay. It's what we need, and we must have our needs met.

Finding the creative in you

How can we let go of perceived and projected negatives and embrace our positives? The creative process can be a very healing, enlightening and immersive experience. Its role is to remind you that kindness and self-acceptance are for you, too. Cultivating a creative practice need not be complicated, nor does it have to become a full-blown interest that you invest a lot of time and money into. It can be as simple as paper and pen and can take a few minutes a day. Or you can dive right in with paint, ink and canvas, getting messy and tactile with the materials you choose. It's not about perfection or 'mastering' it, it's for your enjoyment, pleasure, release and giving yourself the time and permission. There is no need to rush. There is no need to monetise everything you turn your hand or mind to.

As a teenager, I kept a diary and would journal all my experiences and thoughts. Some of my writings back then are cringeworthy to me today, but they were in the moment and who I was then. In my twenties I stopped keeping a journal. One too many stories of sadness and pain, I didn't want to write them down or remember them. As I moved further into my twenties, I took up many art forms because I love creative expression. In my thirties, I returned to journaling with a creative edge—art journaling and writing. I can type way faster than I write so this is often my method of choice. I allow the words to flow and don't read it until I'm done. Often, my writing output is just that: clearing out my thoughts and releasing from my mind whatever is clouding it. There are many words I've written and never re-read because the purpose it served is now complete.

REFLECTION
QUESTIONS

- What were the messages and lessons taught to you while growing up?
- What can you take, leave, learn or even do the opposite of what you internalised?

2
Gutsy Leadership

'If your actions create a legacy that inspires others to
dream more, learn more, do more and become more,
then, you are an excellent leader.'
—Dolly Parton

I have learned a lot about leadership in my forty-five years of living
through observation and *becoming* a leader. The biggest lesson I
have learned is dismantling preconceived patriarchal ideas on what
leadership looks and acts like, and how to show up as the leader YOU
want to be. This is how Gutsy Leadership came into being. Redefining
leadership is the first pillar.

Throughout my career, before I freed myself from the office cubicle
and became an entrepreneur full-time, I observed predominantly one
type of leader: straight, white, middle-aged male—regardless of the
industry or company I worked for. It baffled me on many occasions as
to why this was what a 'leader' looked like, and I quietly questioned why
this was the case when I saw many instances of little brilliance in the
leaders that took up space and dominated management organisation
charts. How could it be that these were the 'best of the best' or 'pick of
the bunch' when it came time for succession planning or recruiting
replacements? Surely there was a Black woman or an Indigenous
person with the skills, experience and qualifications who was capable

of filling these seats and being leaders of teams? Why aren't companies doing anything of note regarding representation, inclusive succession planning and diverse business leadership? Bringing to light the answers to these questions around the boardroom table would shake up the foundations of any white-led, white-dominant workplace, and yet, we know that these questions won't be adequately answered, considered or even contemplated by the status quo leadership unless a Black, Indigenous or Person of Colour with power is sitting at that table. And even then, for those of us who are Black, Indigenous, People of Colour, bringing up such issues could be career suicide. Instead of doing what would be ethical, progressive and equity-driven and focused, the choice to consistently select white leaders to succeed over everyone else is an example of white supremacy in leadership. It's not about skills, experience, qualifications or merit. It's about whiteness choosing whiteness again and again.

Gutsy Leadership invites you to observe, analyse and question all you've been told, shown and conditioned to believe about who the leaders are and who is worthy of leading.

So, what if you don't feel like being a leader because you've been exposed to nothing but white dominance and therefore, white supremacy in leadership? It's no surprise that you would feel like you don't want to be a leader because you feel and can see that the odds are stacked against you. Your social identities differ vastly from those who dominate, so who can you look to for representation inspiration? I understand and I empathise with you, which is why I carved a path of my own to leadership. I took a chance on myself. I didn't plan it this way. I looked right in front of me in the global corporation I worked in, everywhere and in many industries, and it was in activism and social justice that I found leaders who provided the motivation and inspiration I sought. As a Woman of Colour who grew up with limited diverse representation to look up to or towards across all forms of media, it has been so meaningful to me to witness and be part of the diversity of leadership in activism and social justice, to see broad representation of melanated and racialised people, i.e., Black, Indigenous and People of Colour, and to see our numbers increasing in spirituality, coaching and wellness.

A unique way of doing leadership can be found and is possible when we give ourselves permission to claim our leadership potential and inner power. It is within you. It does take more self-trust than, at the time, I was even aware of within myself. I had more faith and trust in myself than I even realised. We are always capable of finding new depths within us. This I know for sure.

In 2015, I began facilitating women's circles and teaching workshops. My first workshop was called Creative Fire and it was a weekend workshop themed 'courage, connection and compassion'. These three things were what my soul craved at the time and what I was growing within myself. This period of facilitating and teaching evolved into Sacred Circle Leadership, the first online program I facilitated to train others to lead and create their own circles, in 2016. At the time, it was all the rage to run women's circles and I enjoyed it so much I wanted to guide others to create circles in their communities, too. One thing that stood out to me was not only the number of women's circles around the world but who was leading them. In my city of Brisbane, I was a rare Woman of Colour leading a circle. At the time, I didn't have the words to articulate or examine why it was that women's circles and spirituality were dominated by white women or that I would find myself one of the very few Women of Colour at white-dominant and white-led events. I quietly asked myself: where are all the Black, Brown, Indigenous and Women of Colour? The answer to that question came a bit later.

My big, bold vision in 2016 was to be an activist and teacher supporting women to create spirals of sisterhood around the globe. A return to ancient traditions where women sat in a circle, sharing, supporting and connecting. To cultivate and create a community of women who, with the support of the circle, would be stronger and braver and more empowered in every area of their lives. Little did I know that what started out as women's circles would become a much bigger vision of Gutsy Leadership and which would lead me to write and teach on the Pillars of Gutsy Leadership, an eight-pillar framework I have implemented and integrated into my business since I wrote the first draft four years ago. Gutsy Leadership itself is leadership, life and business through an anti-racist, anti-oppression and social justice-driven lens. Gutsy Leadership is conscious leadership for now and for the future. It offers thoughts and reflections with the intention of disrupting the status quo where traditional leadership and those who are traditionally seen as leaders are no longer the benchmarks, or as I see it, the low bar setting for leadership. The time for patriarchal notions and default ways of being a leader is over.

What I was noticing, whether it was in my corporate career or in the coaching and spirituality sectors, was not leaders who earned their place on merit, but who got there because the status quo i.e., whiteness, was favoured and upheld as superior and preferred by white society. With this being the symptom of a systemic society, I saw how Gutsy Leadership was different. Gutsy Leadership is conscious and inclusive leadership and inclusive leadership is genuine leadership. Leaders or leadership which excludes the global majority, that is, people who are melanated and racialised—Black, Brown, Indigenous and People of Colour and who do not prioritise the most marginalised or extend space and opportunities to the most marginalised, is not leadership at all. It's white supremacy.

The Pillars of Gutsy Leadership

The Pillars of Gutsy Leadership offers you a framework to become a Gutsy Leader yourself. These are the list of pillars included in related chapters in this book. The first five pillars are covered in this chapter. In relevant chapters, I offer questions for you to explore and reflect on yourself as a leader and your journey and what steps you can take moving forward.

1. Redefine leadership
2. Inclusive leadership is genuine leadership
3. Be the leader you long for
4. Being sovereign

5. Embrace your whole self
6. Tell your stories ('Chapter 11: Writing to Full Expression')
7. Your intuition is your compass (woven throughout)
8. Fierce devotion is an act of self-compassion ('Chapter 15: Becoming You')
9. Real connections and building community ('Chapter 14: Formidable Voices')

Redefining leadership

The first step is to redefine leadership and, as I mentioned at the start of this chapter, this involves dismantling preconceived patriarchal ideas of how leadership acts and what it looks like.

If you've had experiences in white-dominated workplaces you will have some understanding about those who are offered these roles: their traits and behaviours, their management style, their personality and whether inclusion, equity and diversity are factors in their appointment (and therefore embedded in company policies), or in the way they themselves hire employees.

When I first began exploring leadership (and spirituality for that matter), I was confronted with gender binary language everywhere I looked! From researching leadership qualities and traits, I saw these divided into lists about 'male' traits and 'female' traits to 'masculine' and 'feminine' energy in spirituality. Gender binary language is exclusionary and erases those who do not define themselves as a man or woman. It is therefore harmful to use binary language when this is the outcome. Traditional leadership has a bad habit of using gender labels and this needs to stop.

When you think of traditional and patriarchal leadership, that is, straight, white, heteronormative and male-led, what has this form of leadership led you to believe in general? What has traditional and patriarchal leadership led you to believe about yourself and your potential? In what ways, if any, have traditional and patriarchal leadership held you back?

REFLECTION
QUESTIONS

Reflect on some of the leaders you have either worked with or observed in business or in public.

- What are their identities?
- List their race, gender, sexuality, age, class, religion, education level.
- What are their leadership qualities?
- Are they excellent communicators and relationship builders?
- Are they authoritative and domineering?
- Do they practice inclusion? Who do they hire?
- What leadership qualities do you most admire and who has these qualities? What do you look for in a leader?
- If you were to become the leader you long for, what qualities would you possess?
- What traits, gifts, strengths, talents and superpowers do you possess?
- What do others compliment you on?
- What do others come to you for because they value you superpowers?
- What are your leadership values? When you lead, what values are the most important to you?

Can you see how you already possess leadership traits and abilities? Can you see that you are already using these in your daily life?
You are a leader already.

Inclusive leadership is genuine leadership

Leadership is hollow and shallow without inclusivity. It's important to notice who is and who isn't represented in communities and take positive steps to educate yourself about social justice, white supremacy, patriarchy and oppression. Gutsy Leaders do the work to unpack, unravel and unlearn oppressive patterns, beliefs and behaviours. Opting out is not an option. The intention must always be to walk your talk and do the uncomfortable and difficult work on yourself if you are to be authentic in your leadership and be respectful of everyone you encounter. Words have power and meaning when they are followed by integration and action. Acknowledge and recognise marginalisation. It is essential to acknowledge that we don't all start at the same place or have access to the same resources and support.

Meet people where they are but don't lower your core values or your ethics. Become inclusive in the way you live and align your values and beliefs with a Gutsy Leadership lens and ethos.

Lesson of leadership

With the pursuit of inclusive leadership, anti-racism and anti-oppression, comes deep self-awareness and observation of the world. It is a double-edged sword and I'd rather be deep and self-aware than deny or bypass.

After George Floyd was murdered in May 2020, I learned that many people who I thought were on the same page about justice being for all, were not. Some sparse social media comments and calls to action and their activism petered out to nothing when many realised they couldn't profit from being seen as an inclusive person.

In my work, I have taught people to look at themselves first, and attain that self-awareness because it is all too easy to deflect and point the finger at someone else than to address your infallibility. That lesson is one I learned, and I often turn my questions on myself, and it is through this process of questioning that I develop the many questions and prompts I write to help people to work through their beliefs and thoughts.

During 2020, there was a rapid rise in responses to pledges and promises of anti-racism action by numerous non-melanated and non-racialised people, but now in 2022, I ask, like some 90s TV show, where are they now? I have learned that this work has brought me many questions on people's words, behaviour and actions and stems from a lifetime of observing others.

Be the leader you long for

You have so much to offer and already contain everything you need to be a leader. You've seen what traditional leadership looks like, and maybe it has put you off. The time for change has come. Your self-acceptance will allow you as an emerging or seasoned leader to grow and transform and guide others in your own way to their way of being, breaking the old paradigm of traditional leadership and a one-size-fits-only-the-most-privileged approach. Each of us has something to offer and we do things differently. There is no one way.

You own your leadership with grace, inspiring others to accept and re-define theirs. With every 'permission granted' you grow gutsier, and what this world needs is more activated, open, awakened and gutsy people.

I see Gutsy Leadership as a more effective leadership framework because it welcomes open communication, collaboration, sharing of ideas, change and adaptability, and it is not hierarchy-driven. It's an expressive type of leadership that aids personal improvement, elevates performance, is friendlier and inclusive, improves wellbeing and centres authenticity and self-esteem by shining a spotlight on the traits, gifts, strengths, talents and superpowers that a person already possesses. With this view, we are enabling the person to focus on what they have and allow them to bring this brilliance forward with confidence.

The work of the Gutsy Leader

The work of the Gutsy Leader demands devotion and integrity and requires a person to be unwavering and solid on their core values, ethics and boundaries.

It involves taking steps forward to educate yourself about social justice, white supremacy, patriarchy and oppression while knowing this learning is continuous, important and necessary as the world is constantly changing. Gutsy Leaders do the work to unpack, unravel and unlearn oppressive patterns, beliefs and behaviours. A Gutsy Leader knows that opting out is not an option and to bypass an examination of racism and the self is an act of privilege.

Gutsy Leaders are very self-aware people. They notice the big picture and the small details. They have learned that once they see injustice, they will be able to identify it everywhere and will make strides to contribute positively.

Being sovereign

Be sovereign: you are personally responsible and accountable for every one of your choices, beliefs, reactions, decisions, actions and inaction, and addressing what happens in your community spaces. Taking personal responsibility has an impact and knowing the way in which you impact someone is imperative. What does being sovereign mean to you? How might your decisions and choices affect others?

Being sovereign has a caveat: you can't blame anyone. Take ownership of your stuff. You aren't infallible. You are flawed and your acceptance of that, without using it as an excuse, is a lesson in cultivating wisdom. If you fall or fail, learn, educate yourself and strive to do better next time.

Your sovereignty is not in competition with anyone else; your sovereignty compromises no one and vice versa. You taking personal responsibility has an impact and knowing the way in which you impact someone is imperative. Challenge capitalist and patriarchal conditioning when it arises within you.

Gutsy Leadership is about impacting lives in a positive and powerful way, knowing that when you fail at this, it is your responsibility to own it and not put it on someone else. Gutsy Leadership is responsible leadership.

I believe that we grow by falling forwards. It's not failure, it's learning and gaining wisdom. By remembering that our actions, beliefs, motivations, reactions, decisions, choices and inaction have an impact, we can be sovereign from within and not make excuses or bypass responsibility or accountability.

We are capable of breaking patterns and creating new cycles and ways of being and showing up strong and sovereign with our values and integrity.

REFLECTION
QUESTIONS

- What does being sovereign mean to you?
- How have you expressed and shown up as a sovereign leader?
- Remember a time where you didn't take responsibility; what impact did that have?
- Reflect upon a time when you acknowledged your impact and note the outcomes from that wisdom.
- How might your decisions and choices impact others?
- If you haven't been responsible and thoughtful, what might the impact on others be?
- By reflecting on these questions, what have you learned about yourself?

We all have a part to play in the fabric of this world, whether we believe we have power or not. I just know that by forming a collective of people ready to rise, with each person creating a ripple effect of their own, we can bring about the changes this world needs. It may not be pretty, but it will be worth it. It will be messy, painful and difficult, but who are we to claim our position of Gutsy Leaders if we are unwilling to part with some of our privilege to improve conditions for others and take a full-tilt risk, knowing that the benefits for all will outweigh any individual losses?

Activating the Gutsy Leader

It's time to activate the Gutsy Leader within, let's dive in...

Activating Gutsy Leadership is about magnifying *your* innate qualities and talents. The focus is on YOU and what YOU can do. The journey of a leader starts with us. This is where we can align our outer world with our inner world. The journey of collective leadership begins here. I feel that if you make a start on identifying what it is that you can bring forth, you will be able to make adjustments and improvements to your life that will provide you with more of what you want, less of what you don't and the capability and capacity to guide, support and lead others to their greatness.

There are no hard and fast rules, far from it. Gutsy Leadership provides guidance and reflective questions, but your answers come from within. That's your wisdom showing, and it is glorious, innate and ready to beam out! Reflective questions have helped my clients get clarity on their growth, career and business.

Let's get you super clear on your vision and your sacred dream (we all have one or more—this book is one of mine!). Get yourself a pen and paper or your favourite journal (I have seven on the go at once—are you a stationery fiend too?).

Before we get stuck into it, don't be afraid. Your vision can come in all shapes and sizes. It can be squiggly, clear, confusing, enormous or brief and to the point, and that is all okay. You don't have to know it all now, just put down what comes to mind. Slow, deep breaths now.

- What is it you are committed to starting?
- What is your big-picture vision? Map it out, draw it out, write in bullet points, whatever gets it flowing out from you.
- Where is it you will spend my time doing what you love?
- What is it your soul longs to express, do and share with others?
- Are you comfortable with being seen exactly as you are?
- What impact does it have if you aren't comfortable?
- What gets in your way? What holds you back? In what areas do you want to be braver?
- What one thing can you apply today to be seen exactly as you are and for ALL that you are?
- Who can and will support your vision, your mission and your leadership?
- What community and types of people will you need around you to support your vision, mission and leadership?

Why Gutsy?

When we redefine what is 'traditional' and reclaim all that we are without reference to gender, we create an evolved approach to leadership, one that is strong and encouraging, innovative and inclusive, strategic and supportive. When I first came up with Activating Gutsy Leadership in 2015, I called it Activating Feminine Leadership. In whitewashed spirituality, everything was 'masculine' this, 'feminine' that. I adopted this language for a short time, but it was limiting and didn't express the depth of my being or feeling. The limiting binary of masculine and feminine never sat well with me. It was as though this was good enough to use for now because I didn't have the words or knowledge to be more expansive just yet. After learning more about the harm of gender binary language and binaries in general, I ditched the use of 'feminine' from my vocabulary and went with the all-inclusive 'Gutsy'. Now, this felt really good, expansive, welcoming and inviting to all, rather than sticking with the same normative use of language that was at the time inescapable (and, annoyingly, still is today).

Embrace your whole self

You must be willing to embrace all that you are, even if you don't know entirely who you are or what your purpose is. A wealth of knowledge does lie within you. Trust this, even if you don't have all the pieces in place. Question it, too, because there is much to unravel to feel whole. Wholeness is a practice.

Dive deep, dig deep and allow yourself to awaken to your potential. Your triumphs and your mistakes are equally valuable. There's no 'good' or 'bad'. Your liberation will bring liberation to others. Your potential is infinite. Acknowledge and know that your progress through difficult times has so much to offer those drawn to your work and community. Your shadow has a lot to teach you. Open to it, and it will bring you wisdom beyond what you can conceive of now.

An important note

Gutsy Leaders don't have to fit in or be popular. In fact, it's way more fun for a Gutsy Leader to be a rebel, non-conformist, alchemist, sage, mystic, a visionary or a misfit. These are the people drawn to me and to whom I am drawn. You don't have to be anyone but yourself. Discovering who you are is your mission if you desire to take this one life of yours and live it out loud. You don't have to squeeze yourself into little categories or boxes or change who you are to be heard, seen or to matter. People will dislike you anyway, so do you and expand, I say. You already do matter. You are already worthy. You deserve to show up as your genuine self without question, explanation, editing or censorship. This is an entire life mission in itself! So many boundaries, barriers and beliefs to break so that you can begin to feel the freedom of discovering who YOU are.

Have you, throughout your life, been told you were 'too much' or 'too little' of something? I know it is hard not to take it to heart or heave it around like oversized luggage—perhaps for decades because often it is those who raised us or who are closest to us that deliver the sharpest barbs. It's at times like these where The Luggage from Terry Pratchett's *Discworld* novels would come in handy to cart us away from those people. In the novels, The Luggage is a large wooden chest with many little legs and feet, and it is very protective of its owner.

If you are a sensitive rebel, an intuitive visionary or introverted misfit, you might be more susceptible to stinging barbs and outside influences. It can feel like quite the burden. Often those barbs turn into that little voice that tells us we aren't enough, that we are useless, can't do anything or won't amount to anything. I say, enough is enough. Recognising that that voice is not your voice is part of untangling yourself. It's not the pep talk squad, after all, so it's time for you to ditch it and kick it to the kerb. It will take time, but I know that once you can separate your inner voice from the critical voice of others, you will *thrive*. My wish for anyone is to lay to rest the conditioning and messages that hurt us, cause us pain and leave us silent or stuck. We can lay those down and reframe all our muchness and perceived littleness because our muchness is our superpower amongst our bag of tricks. There is nothing little or too much about our superpowers. Those things that irritate, bother, frustrate or cause others discomfort about our traits and personalities (and that lousy people will pick at) will be what draws to us the best people who want to be in our hemisphere, circle and community—those who want to be our peers, friends and partners.

When you devote yourself to a daily practice of silencing those critical inner voices that don't serve us, it will get quieter over time, your true voice will rise above the din. Be patient, love. Your inner voice will get so loud that the *blah blah blah* of criticism won't be easily heard so long as you work on practising self-trust. How funny would it be to respond to the voices of criticism when they are right in front of you, with a hearty, 'We don't have time for any of your blah blah blah. Blah blah blah... blah!' and walk away? I'm feeling that it will feel pretty awesome. I tip my hat to one of my favourite TV shows, *Supernatural*, for that ice-cold quote.

REFLECTION QUESTIONS

- What would a daily practice of self-compassion look like for you?
- What about if you gave yourself a break and turned the self-berating or negative self-talk down? Also, remember, self-talk isn't your inner voice. It's other voices trying to keep you down or stuck.
- What would feel nourishing and nurturing right now?
- What would feel nourishing and nurturing when self-doubt creeps in?

I'd also like to invite you to examine the past four years and how far you've come.
- What have you reclaimed?
- What do you practise?
- What are you learning?
- What are you implementing?
- What are you embodying?
- What have you learned by integrating lessons into your being, life, career and/or business?
- What does wholeness feel like to you? Open up into full sensory mode. What does it look like? What's present there? What does it sound like/smell like/taste like?
- How does it feel to embrace your whole self?
- What would it mean to feel whole?
- What would it mean to be whole?

3
Reclaiming Me

'The only dream worth having is to dream that you
will live while you are alive, and die only when you are
dead. To love, to be loved.'
—Arundhati Roy

Reclaiming

This world is hard enough as it is without continuing to tell people
that you have a greater right to define them than they do themselves.
I don't seek perfection on the path, though I am pretty hard on myself
to get it—whatever it may be—right. Once I knew it was essential to
becoming gutsy, reclaiming myself has been necessary, hard, painful,
transformative and deliberate. I continue to be a work in progress for
my whole life. It gets pretty loud in my brain and nobody is paying rent
in here but me, so it is a work in progress to kick out the freeloader
tenants in my brain.

Labels of identity

Gender binary language is harmful. It was 2016 when I became friends
with Cameron Airen and hired them for a gender consultation.

Cameron Airen is now co-founder of Feminist Coach Academy with my friend Naomi Arnold. I was curious to learn how I was doing with my communications and inclusion regarding gender. I wanted to ensure that my communication and inclusive practice was reflecting my values on gender identity. Cameron helped me to make the necessary updates, which didn't amount to very much because I was already largely living my beliefs and values around inclusion and, specifically, gender identity.

This was the early phase of becoming inclusive in my life and work, as I unpacked my very foundations and conditioning to question labels of identity. I'd also had question marks regarding my sexuality for some time, but in 2016 I wasn't ready to go down that road, yet.

The changes I was making to Gutsy Leadership began with gender and removing 'feminine' and 'masculine' from the whitewashed spirituality vocabulary I was ridding myself of.

I don't believe being adamant about only using gender binary language is kind and inclusive, it's harmful and awful. The way people will hold fast to the gender binary like their lives depend on it when it has never been *their* lives at stake has ceased to amaze me. I am no longer shocked at people's shallow depths of self-enquiry, failing to examine their bias, hatred, beliefs, conditioning and behaviours. This is the kind of pigheadedness that has traumatised many marginalised identities.

I detest the excuses people give for refusing to use someone's preferred pronouns and/or name. Mine are they/she, by the way. My consultation with Cameron led me to decide my pronouns, to be more descriptive about gender inclusion and who my work and spaces are for, and to clearly communicate that there was no room for anyone to enact harm regarding gender identity or sexuality in my spaces and work.

Of all the topics I teach and facilitate, gender identity has been one of the most uncomfortable, difficult and hardest to guide people in making a shift. In life coaching, spirituality and wellness industries, gender binary language is woven into marketing, about pages, sales pages and FAQs which continue to uphold the whitewashed masculine and feminine energy descriptions and programs and events 'just for women'.

When I began to integrate what I was unlearning about gender, I wrote this on my website: 'I don't use the words "feminine" or "masculine" to describe energy, bodies, traits or myself. Binary thinking and language erases and excludes, and I am not here for that.'

If you do not define yourself by the gender binary, your exclusion, your invisibility is immediate. Basically, if you are non-binary, queer, trans, agender, the message is that these spaces will not have you (nor are they safe). When I sat with that thought and with my experiences of not belonging, not fitting in, doing my 'am I the only melanated person in the room?' headcount, I knew I wouldn't want to be a part of those programs and events anyway, even if they did change their language to be more inclusive overnight, because being inclusive by nature isn't an instant or overnight integration event. It happens and evolves slowly as you, the individual, is untangling from all that has conditioned you, unpacking your privilege and then taking action based on depth, understanding and learning undertaken over a period of months and years, not days. It happens only when you want to untangle. You will cross paths with people, as I have, who have benefited so strongly from upholding the gender binary, that they'll never want to see an end to it when they can profit from being 'feminine', 'alpha male' etc. The challenge is when you know and believe that the gender binary is harmful and oppressive and you discover that people you like or people who you have paid for products and services uphold and defend the gender binary, or worse, put out hateful content against trans and non-binary people. Will you be complicit by continuing to support and stay connected to those people?

Aren't we human?

I identify as human before any other label. If you meet me at that place first and do not label or judge me as you see fit based on my appearance, then we might begin to create some history together. In 2021, I had some big conversations with close friends about identity only to realise on some level that we were all examining or questioning labels we had adopted or grown used to. It's kind of sad to acknowledge that one identity I've been ascribed to for all of my adult life—woman—isn't one I feel connected to anymore, and I can partially thank whitewashed spirituality for this.

My time avidly absorbing the gospel according to privileged white women was thankfully short before I started to question everything I was reading, noticing and hearing. I recognised formulas and patterns and, for me, I began to identify what wasn't for me. During 2013 and 2017, I read one too many bestselling books by said writers and never felt satisfied, better off or more informed by the end of them. All I felt each time was, *I can't relate to any of this, that passed some time: next.* One of the very last spiritual self-help bestsellers I read set off already active trauma which was a painful year-long experience. I could laugh nervously about it or be thankful that it 'unlocked' something, but I won't. It was serious and it was a lesson learned, and a caution to be discerning about who I was reading and learning from. I still had another year to go before I would really declutter and grow more discerning. I was so sick of seeking substance, paying for it and coming up with nothing. It felt like that at that time and some of who I was reading made it very clear that their self-awareness was nowhere near the depths I would expect from a leader or the depths I would go to myself. It was also clear to me that their excessive reliance on culturally appropriative practices and tools was something they were contently profiting from—and don't even think about calling that out. I can't recall all of the books now as I discarded them in 2017 when I decluttered my bookshelf and replaced them all with social justice writers, activists and academics, melanated witches and brujas.

This journey of identity exposes many things including what

I thought about identities I'd ascribed to. 'Woman' being the most obvious one before you even meet my eyes or see my skin. Some descriptive identities have served me, others have served to reduce me, other me or displace me, and often more than one at a time, which is no mean feat. I want to express this as simply and plainly as possible so you can flip it on yourself and consider how it would feel for you if someone were to 'overrule' your expression of identity claiming they know what yours is better: I am not whatever gender you think I should be. I am human and I identify as a biracial human. I am also a mother.

REFLECTION
QUESTIONS

- What are your identities?
- How do you define yourself?
- What are your current thoughts and beliefs regarding gender identity?
- What is inclusion to you?
- What are you noticing about whitewashed spirituality that doesn't resonate with you any longer?
- What are the messages being communicated and why?
- What is the benefit for you?

Being biracial

In early 2018, I began writing a series on being biracial for my now closed Patreon (I've since moved to ko-fi). Through a series of four posts, I explored my experiences, thoughts and reflections on my life as a biracial human, this is how I describe myself nowadays. I brought this writing into the book to talk about identity and to share my thoughts and experiences on being biracial.

Being biracial: part one

My personal experience of being biracial has been complicated. When I was growing up there was no one, not even anyone in my family, who looked like me. I am an only child. My father is Northern Irish and my mother is Chinese-Indonesian. I was born in and grew up in Sydney, Australia.

My earliest experience of racism was when I was in primary school in the school yard when a bout of name-calling slurs occurred. The next I can recall was when boarding a bus with my ma, and an older man verbally abused us about going 'back to your own country'. I witnessed my mother be overlooked in shop queues and recall one instance when I was probably eleven or twelve where I raised my voice to the counter staff declaring that my mother was next in line.

In my teenage years I experienced regular, growing-to-daily racial abuse at school. Snide comments, jibes and provocation for a reaction. Unfortunately for me, I always reacted. I was always on alert. I had regular feelings of dread when I spotted the people who wanted me to suffer. I can't tell you the number of boys I slapped in the face after they hurled slurs at me; I lost count. This frequent experience wore me down. No wonder I found it difficult to concentrate on schoolwork when I was constantly depleted from being on guard all the time.

At school, I didn't feel like I belonged. I didn't know anyone who experienced racism in the same way. We were young and never spoke about it. I knew that I wasn't then able to articulate all that was happening and how it made me feel. I was regularly told that I wasn't Australian. I started to believe it. I started to believe that despite being born in this country, where my parents worked hard to build a life for us through working in aged care, factories and on the land, I was better off having no allegiance to this place that:

1. Didn't respect or value its First Nations population.
2. Continues to discriminate against migrants to this day.

Even though we are all migrants with the exception of First Nations people. Why would I want to identify as Australian if this was the attitude of its people?

I'm olive skinned, with black hair and dark brown eyes—my mother's colouring. Tall and skinny, with hands, feet and limbs like my dad and a narrow-bridged nose that I'd call unique. 'Where do I belong?' I often asked myself.

I grew up seeking, looking for role models and representatives in magazines and other media who I could relate to. The search was often unsuccessful. The internet didn't come into mainstream use until after I left high school in 1994. In 2023, we are seeing more efforts for greater diversity and representation. It would be an understatement for me to say that this is a long time coming, but there is still a lot more that needs to change to embed diversity, equity and inclusion into everyday life. These are necessities, and diversity, equity and representation must be proactive and not an afterthought.

When I travelled overseas to my parental homelands, I felt a resonance to the land, but by appearance I didn't 'fit'. Too olive and Asian-eyed to be Irish, too tall (5'8") and light-skinned to be Chinese-Indonesian. When I was in Indonesia, little old ladies no taller than my upper arm would approach me at the market, touching my arm and skin as though I was from another world.

Being asked where I am from (mostly by Caucasians, I might add) is a tedious question where I notice that, in the thousands of times I've been asked, I immediately feel 'other' to the person asking, that feeling of not belonging rearing its unfortunate head yet again. I take a deep breath, or I sigh or pause and look them directly in the eye asking, 'what do you mean exactly?'. At the time of writing this in 2018, I was asked one morning by someone at my office! Eye rolling and exaggerated brow furrowing may also be part of my response. These conversations come to a standstill, and I turn icy if I'm complimented on my English, or if there are remarks about them 'not seeing colour' or any reference to yellow or 'exotic'.

I have an Australian-flavoured accent that to some doesn't sound like other Australians or Australian at all. I guess that is what happens when your father retains his Northern Irish accent and your mother has accented English. A hybrid accent of no fixed address, region or location.

I didn't learn how to speak Indonesian until I was twenty-three. The office I was working for at the time closed and we were all made redundant. I chose to invest my redundancy in an Indonesian Language and Culture program, a partnership between The University of Sydney and Universitas Kristen Satya Wacana in Central Java, Indonesia. I wanted to reclaim and connect with my culture, so I travelled to Indonesia, stayed with family, travelled around Java and Bali and lived in a town of 100,000 people for a time and learned Bahasa Indonesia and regional culture. My mother's language is actually Sundanese, the native language of the ethnic group of the same name. Incidentally, 'sunda' derives from the Sanskrit prefix su- meaning goodness.

When I was growing up, my mother was learning to speak English and assimilating into Australian life in our uniquely blended family of three (the first of my 'trinities'). We both lost out. She lost her connection to her culture and language on a daily basis, and I lost out on learning her dialect and, to this day, am unable to speak with most of my relatives in Indonesia. Our identities are compromised because that is the price that is paid when you live in the 'West'. You *must* fit in, you *must* assimilate and your language is not acceptable to be spoken in public. That's the message I felt in my youth, and it is a message that continues for many other people today as Australia has grown more diverse with over 300 languages spoken.[1]

Being biracial: part two

In 2018, I combed through my unpublished blog and while perusing posts from 2014–2016, lo and behold, I could see how persuasive whitewashed spirituality was with its Law of Attraction/The Secret/Abraham-Hicks, love 'n light and spiritual bypassing hooks. Looking back now, I can see how I enabled them to stall my growth, spiritual and otherwise, and how what I was exposed to would become part of my undoing and my reclaiming. After a few years of intuitive art practice, art journaling and exploring in my creative cave (and a lifetime of searching for myself), you know, doing my own thing of inner excavation and doing okay, albeit slowly, I began to follow lifestyle bloggers and self-styled new thought leaders and gurus promoting a way of self-love and an empowerment that had a big drawcard for me at the time: sisterhood. Through these people, I came to engage with the work of *The New York Times* Best Sellers and entrepreneurs peddling their brands of capitalism who, on reflection, wore an invisibility cloak when it came to understanding intersectionality. Upon serious examination of their work and myself, I realised they were not speaking to me. Definitely not to me. But my dollars, oh, they liked those.

What I was hearing then spoke to aspects of myself at the time—a twenty-year-plus professional career and salary to match (though no university degree), private health insurance, life insurance and the ability to invest in myself and my personal development by buying their books, programs, talks and workshops. They were selling a dream achieved by few: 'Follow what I do and you, too, can be an author, speaking on global stages, living a luxe life with shiny brand photos and laughing yourself all the way to the bank'. They are not informed or qualified to address multiple traumas, mental health or racism because these experiences are not in their bio or backstory. They can't teach you what they do and how to do it and why, because they don't have your full story in mind, they don't need to. I recognised that they were speaking to unawakened parts of myself that had me believing that the playing field was equal and speaking to the parts of myself that were ingrained in internalised oppression.

Beyond the sale of sisterhood, I didn't want what they were selling. I didn't actually want fake and shiny. I don't want fake friends or fake smiles or shiny experiences lacking substance. What I do want is to share my words and write from my heart with depth and help people in ways unlike what was being marketed to me. I want to help people break free of these so-called 'laws' and principles, to choose their own path, adopt critical thinking skills and logic, and form some trust in their intuition and to question every message they are taking in. I vowed not to twist anyone's hearts with promises of miracles from 'manifesting', only to then blame them for bringing negativity, doom and gloom into their lives when things didn't work out as directed. I swore I wouldn't simply tell people to 'be positive' as if that were a recipe for real change or recovery from a life-threatening illness or situation.

I want to be my weird self, raw and real, and not hide any part of who I am. I want a simple, safe and comfortable life, and I want that for other people, too. I don't want to be on a pedestal, and I most certainly do not want to be a guru. That shit is scary, and I baulk at anything with cult vibes.

I read many books in my young adulthood on cults because I was curious about human thoughts, behaviours and beliefs and wanted to understand what made these cult gurus create what they created and why people were mesmerised by them. In whitewashed spirituality, cult vibes are present and vary from gushing fangirling to idolatry and reliance on this idolised individual to solve or cure their problems.

I discovered that all of these systems, processes, strategies, ten-point plans, methodologies and principles being peddled were not working for me. I felt awful. I looked outside myself because I was desperately seeking and what I found was wrong for me in the end. I fucking tried. I busted my arse for those years trying to use their systems, allowing their stylish social media feeds, glowing head shots and persuasive words rooted in patriarchy and femininity to twist my thinking to the point that I thought that I wasn't working hard enough (because another twenty to thirty hours a week doing my own thing ON TOP of my then full-time job while also being a wife AND mother wasn't enough?), that I didn't want it enough, that I was somehow 'low vibe', that I invited assault/abuse/bullying/racism as part of my karmic lessons and was the sole saboteur to blame for my lack of perceived 'success'.

I chose to believe the lies back then—every single one, and now I'm fired up. I'm awake now and my invitation to you is to question who is preaching to you, who is persuading you, who wants your money, who wants your adulation, who is and isn't here for you and to help you to untangle your beliefs from the webs they've woven into your psyche. I know that's not me and maybe that's not you either. It's not their fault, they're within the oppressive systems too and they have greatly benefited and profited from them, and they know it. How do we know they know? Well, we know because in recent years when more and more calls for real change and justice have multiplied, they aren't at the frontline backing up people less privileged than themselves. They might step in if they think they can get something out of it, and then they peel off never to raise the subject again. They know how these oppressive systems work because everything they continue to do helps them to reap the rewards and benefits. If they wanted to change, for the world to be more inclusive, for the world to be less oppressive, they'd be putting muscle behind it with every ounce of privilege they have, and we know that's not happening, right? Their money's on the line and, as I've written elsewhere before, a capitalist never makes a change unless it positively affects their bottom line. All of these oppressive systems work seamlessly together. Realising what you are tangled in takes awareness, learning and an investment in your time to use logic and critical thinking to untangle yourself from it.

Your life is not a game of Monopoly and neither is mine, nor the melanated people in our communities. Intersections matter and I have made it an intention of mine over the years to promote, support, share, encourage and choose to work only with people who share my values on dismantling and extracting ourselves from these systems. To align, stay connected or get to know only those who are actively learning, who are doing the damn work, occasionally stumbling, but doing what they can. Making mistakes is part of unravelling internalised oppression and racism. If you aren't making mistakes, if you aren't open to learning, how can you fathom or picture being in another's shoes or empathise with their life experiences so far?

Being biracial: part three

Being biracial, being both Asian and white and having my name means I am constantly feeling under attack from white women (and men!) who take offence to my calling in and calling out, and melanated women who are fired up and prepared to jump on anyone that does not look 'brown enough' in their view. Justifying my existence is exhausting. I always check, double check, ask and really discover before jumping to conclusions. Unfortunately the same courtesy is not always afforded to me.

Living in Australia, I'm one of very few biracial Asian people who have been working in the coaching and spirituality spaces, which are severely whitewashed. It's a pretty lonely existence, let me tell you. When I go into shared and melanated-only online spaces, I'm again one of the very few and being questioned or using eye roll emoticons in response because I'm not seen for my identity. I've had to repeat my identity constantly, and often to the same people! I identify as Biracial Asian. I have made it public knowledge as much as possible, but it is a daily battle. I get the feeling each time I'm about to post or comment in a group, the 'here we go, brace yourself, it's going to happen again'. It makes me feel like withdrawing, like doing this work solo, posting and sharing on my own pages only and not contributing in communities because sooner or later, someone is going to tell me off instead of asking and not recognising the inference of my identity in what I post. I'm tired today. I'm tired every day from the battle to be seen for forty-one years, three months and a few days...

Representation matters

In my life, in 2018, I'm fed up. I'm fed up with total lack of representation in spaces I want to be in, on the stage, in the media and on store shelves. I feel like this recent new moon kicked up a fire that has long been brewing in me—to speak openly and honestly about how I feel about the total lack of equitable representation of women and melanated people in the spiritual entrepreneurial community.

Truthfully, I feel fucking duped. Duped by spiritual communities here and overseas. I feel duped because even though I knew I was different and I look different, it didn't occur to me that with my bag of trauma and racism swag, that the whitewash and love 'n light stuff wouldn't be effective processes or practices to help me get free from the burden because they are taught by non-melanated and non-racialised people who have not experienced anything close to what I have. What I have come to know is I had to dismantle it all, from the books and whitewashed oracle cards I bought, to the blogs I read, the programs I paid for and get for free by, well, being true to me in a gutsier and greater sense than the 'be true to yourself woo woo' carbon copy crew.

Sometimes it seems like it's a 'who you know' situation or 'let's make up the numbers because, hey, marketing strategy for the win!'. Though, often, the community is so whitewashed it wouldn't know what to do with someone who had truly ancient ancestral wisdom or someone who has experienced prolonged racial bullying. In fact, it has always, always, always been easier for non-melanated and non-racialised people to ignore or pretend that they don't see differences in colour, ethnicity, race, etc., yet they are the very same people who ask you incessantly 'where are you from?', 'noooo, where are REALLY from?'. I could ask, what do you do at traffic lights or how do you pick your shellac at the salon? I digress. It wouldn't know that Law of Attraction is a steaming pile of victim blaming, spiritual bypassing you-know-what for anyone who is on the margins. It wouldn't know that donning a bright wig and lipstick is not going to make you feel any better about being on food stamps, welfare or not being able to pay your medical bills. I mean, *isn't there an oil for all that?*

Truth is, the spiritual entrepreneurial community is not that awake. It groggily has just one eye open so long as the positive vibes roll on in and you keep paying by the thousands and you don't start spouting how social justice IS spiritual and is a huge piece of conscious spiritual leadership. You lose followers for that in droves. This I know.

Don't get me wrong, I exist with some privileges: I have a roof over my head (renting), healthcare (different and much cheaper than the

USA) and a professional job, but I feel that the realities of people from all walks of life hardly get a mention or more than a sad face from those who front the spiritual community, as thought leaders and self-styled gurus, who spout messages of self-care from their laptop lifestyles wearing yoga pants made from PET bottles. It's time we got real about how exclusionary the spiritual community is, how any shred of negative thought or feeling is brushed over or lit up with love 'n gaslighters and people crying 'it's not my fault I'm white'.

I'm unpacking a lot about identity for myself and the deeper I get into it, the more 'other' I feel. I have read several stories on biracial and multiracial people and no matter our unique stories, there are common threads and feelings. Many of the ways they felt like they didn't belong could have been written by me.

Being biracial: part four

There is very little reciprocity on racial understanding, minimisation of harm and empathy. This lack of cross-cultural understanding and, let's be honest, effort, by white counterparts is why relationships become estranged once the race conversation comes across the table after years of silence. One ends up biting one's tongue and keeping the peace to keep non-melanated and non-racialised people comfortable and, ironically, 'on side'. Ask any melanated person and they'll have numerous examples of silence, the outrage when we speak up and the constant racial aggressions, language, jokes and stereotypes we've endured against ourselves and other melanated people.

My view is that if you are racist and prejudiced against one racial identity, it's a spit in the face to all of us. I don't abide by any racism towards any racialised and melanated people. I often feel like the measure of someone's humanity is tied to how they speak to and about others who live in a different skin. Likewise, empathy and respect.

If you're new to this topic, please note: racism against non-melanated and non-racialised people? Nope. Get Google ready.

Life is easier for non-melanated and non-racialised people when we (the melanated) erase our racial identities and continue to allow them to live in the daydream of a world where they 'don't see colour'. When they don't see colour, they don't see the fullness of us and when they don't see AND accept the fullness of us, not only are they missing out on who we are at our deepest levels, they are choosing to sideline our humanity for their comfort.

I won't be part of that anymore and that's why in recent years so many relationships have lapsed, become estranged or distant because I deserve more than to put my body and identities on the line for white comfort, whether those relationships are blood kin or otherwise. I am a big believer and doer when it comes to self-responsibility and sovereignty. I believe in owning my shit, taking responsibility, being accountable and not doing harmful shit again, and that means I have high expectations of others because I hold myself one-hundred-percent accountable. I'm tough on myself and have perfectionist tendencies. I practise what I preach. Actions are what I look at, not just someone's words. People can be all talk and zero action and I'm not one to let things slide. This is the way I am and because of it I've been called intimidating, and that projection is an example of other people's lack of self-awareness and personal responsibility and inability to recognise personal power in another without feeling like my existence is a threat to their tranquillity. My view is: I'll start keeping the peace when you make peace with self-awareness and owning what's yours.

Evoking boundaries and learning how to set them have been big pieces of my learning and development, in parallel to accepting myself wholly and becoming anti-racist in all areas of my life. Long before I knew there was a name for it, I prophesied reactions to my call outs about racist language and jokes. Non-melanated and non-racialised people online didn't disappoint when it came to defensive behaviour and whitesplaining themselves deeper into the racist holes they expertly dug. I have ruminated on ways I might tackle the whole minefield moving forward, knowing there are far too many people who really don't know me in my personal life and who still try to educate me on race when I call for accountability or state that what someone is saying is harmful and wrong. It's truly laughable that some kin have no idea I have made a life and business since 2017 being an anti-racist and anti-oppression writer, speaker and coach. I have paid various prices for that, but ultimately, I'm glad that I have backed myself.

What I have experienced has sucked the compulsion to educate non-melanated and non-racialised people in my personal life when get-togethers occur. Over the years, I have dreaded how the more my learning has expanded and my tolerance for racist bullshit has declined, it has meant I have to prepare for encounters on mental, emotional and energetic levels. I really have to hold myself, practise vigilance and be prepared for whatever shit is bound to come out of people's mouths, and it is my job to develop better boundaries and not allow the nasties in.

One method I'll employ from now on is far more dramatic than I am as a person, but I trust it'll be effective, and I do expect an Oscar miniature for this: leaving the room, leaving the house, whoever's it is, and driving away. No explanation needed. I'm yet to try this to see what happens. Who knows? By the time this book is in print, I may even have a story to share on its effectiveness.

Objectification, scrotums and boob rankings

The objectification and experiences of sexism and body commentary from the male gaze began early in my life. I was a lean kid with knobbly knees who experienced comments, judgement and critique about my body and size. In the height of world hunger awareness in the 1980s, a boy who continued to be a nemesis all the way through to year 12 made comments on my small frame, teasing and asking if I was Ethiopian. Already the murmuring of veiled racism and anti-Blackness (even though I'm not Black) was coming out and directed at me. I was in grade 2. We never played *Star Wars* in the schoolyard ever again. The first boundary I was building was 'under construction'.

My pre-menstruating body was called 'sexy' by boys who had just entered their teens and yelled it out of the bus window at me in the afternoon as I walked home from school. I was in year 7. I recall the embarrassment and humiliation of finger-pointing boys who ranked my friends and my attractiveness according to our breast size. I was ranked last by these boys, half of whose scrotums hadn't even dropped yet. Obviously, I was yet to develop the art of the snappy comeback. I was in year 8.

It was around this time boys began calling me 'Ana', short for anorexic. I never had an eating disorder and didn't develop one despite this constant objectification and degrading commentary about my body. I was teased for wearing glasses which I began wearing in grade 4 because I strained to read my teacher's writing on the blackboard from the back of the classroom.

In the story of *Red Jumper, Blue Jeans* that follows, I came to realise that this was just the beginning of the shallow depths of patriarchal and misogynistic waters I'd have to tread for many years to come. One thing was clear to me then: these boys were not being taught any other way to be in their households. It was 'boys will be boys' against us gendered girls whose self-confidence and beliefs had already taken a beating as early as primary school. What choice did we have other than to tread water in this toxic filth of patriarchy and pray that it didn't drown us?

REFLECTION
QUESTIONS

- Which of your stories will set you free?
- Which stories have you avoided or not addressed?
- What parts of yourself can you reclaim and begin to heal from?
- Who are your trusted loved ones?
- Who do you feel safe to tell your story to?
- What have you learned about self-acceptance?
- What have you learned about boundaries?

- What boundaries will you set for yourself?
- What friendships and relationships are no longer worth your love, time and energy?
- Write a letter of compassion to your younger self.

4
Undone

'I have this theory of convergence, that good things always happen with bad things. I know you have to deal with them at the same time, but I just don't know why they have to happen at the same time. I just wish I could work out some schedule.'
—Diane in *Say Anything* (1989)

*This chapter contains references to sexual assault and rape.

Beginnings

I wish I could tell you that healing, self-discovery and finding the truest version of yourself was a straight-lined journey filled with easy-to-access gateways, roads and portals that follow one after the other. I can't lie. It's got a little of that, and so much more. Let me begin by saying it will be worth it. You are worth discovering yourself. You are worth the time and investment in healing. You are worth it even when you say no because your boundaries are important.

Whether you are at the beginning, the recent messy middle like me or the beyond-belief best version of yourself with no regrets and no looking back, may my words be salve when things get crispy, tough, hard and you want to flake out of life and out of sight. They are paths I've been on, too. These challenges and obstacles along the way are beyond the physical. They are emotional, mental and spiritual, too. I wish I had a better understanding of all of that earlier in life—but no regrets—I have learned to work with what I've got and resource myself as needed.

In my work I talk and write a lot about honouring the self, honouring your time, energy, capacity and boundaries. Cultivating the self-respect to believe and deeply know that you are worth the effort is a parallel journey. We face the paradoxes of our existence, how we can feel happy but unhappy on the inside, how we can be thrilled for someone's wonderful news and silently wishing we could be further along one of our many paths.

There's a moment when you bring the emotional and mental and spiritual into the physical. I do this with breathwork techniques I've learned over the years and noticing how my body speaks to me if I quieten everything else and just be within myself.

This is how I do it: I get really still and connect with myself. I do a few stretches, shakes, dance a bit, or get up on my bed and do an enormous full-bodied cat stretch, roll and twist, releasing tension and feeling my cells tingle. Scalp massage and heat packs on my body where needed help, too. Move. Notice what feels good and repeat. Then I stop and take deep breaths, feeling my belly fill up, holding for a few seconds, then exhaling. I notice what is happening in my body and I ask: how does this time, space and presence feel when I allow myself?

Red Jumper, Blue Jeans, 12 Nov 2021

This is what I was wearing when I was first assaulted by a boy who put his hand down my top without my consent. It was humiliating and not funny like he and his friends thought. They laughed and teased me at school afterwards and I did my best to not let the pain and humiliation show on the outside. Is this what becoming resilient was?

The second time it happened, I was wearing much the same. I can't remember. It's one small detail of this particular day that I cannot recall. Sometimes I wish what I was wearing was the only thing I could remember, but that's not the reality.

On this second occasion, it was that same year 10 boy and one of his friends and they held me down. It wasn't a game. It was terrifying. I couldn't believe this was happening. It was aggressive and a violation of my body. They wrestled me to the floor and held me down by my wrists and ankles. I struggled to break free, but it was no use. I froze in fear, no sound came out.

I will never forget that terror as my then-friend and her boyfriend looked on. Neither of them made a move to come to my aid beyond my friend taking one step forward. My friend's boyfriend gestured to her to stay put. I will never forget their faces and expressions. My friend's boyfriend grinned while it was happening. I will never forget my friend's betrayal. It remains with me today.

What they did to me—it was a joke to these year 10 boys. I was fourteen and in year 8. It happened in a public place and all I could think of in those moments of panic and fear was that I was worried that someone would walk in on what was happening.

The pain I felt from their laughter and glee was a double blow and added to my memory of the trauma, fear and pain I experienced that day.

What we wear has nothing to do with why someone makes the choice to be a sexual offender or rapist. It doesn't stop them from being who they are and taking advantage of a moment in time where they feel entitled to steal a piece of our bodies.

It's never about what we wear or what we say or do, it's about their entitlement, desire to dominate, overpower, disrespect, humiliate and declare that they are boys and men and can do whatever the fuck they like with little or no repercussions or punishment.

I didn't report it. I didn't tell my parents. I was locked in my cage of shame for the decades that followed, disconnected from my body, pained. I already knew how these things played out and I would be denied my humanity. My friend and I spoke no more about it, and I continued as though everything was fine. It wasn't and I wasn't.

Over two decades later when on the journey of personal development and healing and facing my trauma, I sought some semblance of peace for that painful day.

Peace for myself that I was not a victim, but a survivor.

Peace for myself that I didn't have to continue to keep this secret.

Peace that I was worthy of being respected.

Peace that I didn't have to continue hating, loathing or blaming myself for what had been done to me.

I was a part of this without my consent.

I was only in text contact with that former friend through my twenties. One day I messaged her to tell her how I had not forgotten her face or her inaction. She asked me if I blamed her and the hurt, memory of abandonment and broken trust flooded back. It was suffocating. I grieved my fourteen-year-old self. My former friend apologised for her part in not coming to my aid and I left it at that because we were no longer friends.

None of that brought me peace, just grief and loss for the girl I could've been had these events not happened, had someone been there to protect and help me. I learned that I had to be my protector and that added another layer to my complexity as a human being and my 'unspoken demands' when it came to friendships and relationships. When lines were crossed, I left. Sometimes I was weak enough to return because I didn't value or respect myself. I learned that later.

A tapestry of trauma is woven through my story. I,

however, am not my trauma. On my path of peace and healing I learned this to be true. I am not my trauma. I want you to know this if my story resonates or is similar to yours: you aren't your trauma, either.

I was on a path of seeking my peace and overcoming how I hated myself so much. In future relationships I let myself be mistreated, used, disrespected and I thought the cycle would never end. But it did because I found the love of a man who lived the values of respecting others, who was loyal and loves, respects and defends me more than I ever thought I would deserve.

I blamed myself for a long time and kept the memory shoved back in my mind as far as I could for twenty-two years, before I found the courage to share my experience in detail with my partner and best friend. Their support and love guided me to believe I was worthy of seeking professional help.

On that same day of confessing what I kept hidden, I made the unfortunate mistake of also telling someone, a close former work friend who I thought I could trust. Their response was the exact opposite of support and compassion. It was so unexpected after the support and care I had provided her during our friendship when she was being stalked by a female colleague we had worked with. I will never forget her words in the email she sent me after I revealed to her at the time, my deepest trauma: 'I'm not your counsellor'.

Our friendship came to a sudden end that day and changed my boundaries and the way I engaged in future close friendships with highly privileged cis-hetero white women.

When the trust was broken or lines and boundaries were crossed, I would slam the door on a friendship forever. I refused to be hurt by them ever again and ending the friendship was my only choice. Life was too short to stay friends with people who hurt, harm and take from us. Reciprocity became a non-negotiable value in my friendships with women from that point onward.

Back then, I wish I knew the wisdom and self-worth that would come with age and the power of seeking help and allowing people who love me to have my back. I wish I knew the strength I had within me that was always there but unrealised in my teenage years.

I can write about this now as though I'm narrating a story and, while it is mine, I have moved through most of the painful emotions it brings up.

These traumatic experiences of assault do not define me, but they do shape my story, my values, boundaries and how I show up as a human, coach, advocate, activist and friend today.

I was trying to cope with so much as a teenager: racism, bullying, sexism, misogyny, decisions about my future, self-loathing, self-belief, not belonging, being disconnected from my body and shoving sexual trauma down—and that's not even a complete list.

It was too much to contemplate, face and accept myself at all, and that I was bisexual then just as much as I am now, since coming out to a select few people in 2018, and being more public about my identity since then.

There was just no room for all of me.

I had to learn to accept myself so that I could heal the hurts.

Maybe you'll now understand how hard it was to put these stories into words, to reflect on and retell painful parts of my experience and story, but I felt I must share them because these experiences shaped who I was to become.

Once I finally wrote Red Jumper, Blue Jeans in late 2021, I crashed. I felt relieved that finally these words were on the page. I felt deep pain, sorrow, grief and loss for many reasons that, at the time of finishing this chapter, I am still processing, attempting to be gentle with myself and recognise that I'm okay, today.

I'm reminded of the deep pain for fourteen-year-old me again. Sorrow, grief and loss for all the years this story burdened and traumatised me into silence, the years that would, in my mind, have been 'better' without this baggage. None of what happened can be taken back, apologised for or reversed by returning to the past. It's a part of me and my story that I've reclaimed through its telling. This trauma does not hold me back, not since I faced it head-on in therapy in 2013. This trauma does not control me as it once did.

I call upon my strength and grit and ask, WHO has the power now? Bitch, I do.

No matter what your story is, whether it is told or hidden or you're still processing, trying to move forward and/or healing, I believe that you are capable someday of reclaiming your whole self, body, mind, soul and story. Not just because I did, but because loving myself wholly, fully, and moving towards self-acceptance have been some of the greatest necessities I've needed to anchor into to tell you my story.

A love letter for all the times you didn't fight back

Dear younger me,

I wish I wrote you this letter decades ago. You didn't know what you didn't know back then. It's okay.

You fought as hard as you could with what you had. It confused you. You are a sensitive soul who observed so much and took it all in but didn't have the words. You didn't know who it was that you would become. I want you to know that you do now. You grew up and I'm proud of who you have become. You were raised to be kind, caring and generous and often those traits were taken advantage of and you beat yourself up so hard.

I'm so sorry the world and your emotions confused and confounded you so much. It will take you quite some time to gain clarity on all of it, but trust me, you will get there. Turn that kindness, care and generosity to yourself. Life is going to be a wild, scary ride and you won't feel like you belong anywhere for a long time. You will have to make places of belonging for yourself. You will spend a lot of time alone and you will love that you can craft an inner world where you are safe and can experience richness through all your passions and obsessions. You will have to find friends and lovers who elevate you and make you feel safe. This, too, will take a while, but it will happen, and it will be all you wish for and more. It's okay to be confused. It's okay to be angry when things don't work out and when relationships break down.

Beating yourself up will cause you to internalise a lot of pain and take on other people's emotions until you learn how to be with yourself. You will have to make different choices and sometimes it will be hard to choose yourself above everything else. Everything life throws at you, you will rise up from.

Please believe it, and trust me, your wildest, most impossible dream will come true.

With love,
You, age forty-five.

A love note for the deeply feeling and emotionally sensitive

You may feel like you are an emotional time bomb about to go off.
Repressing emotions harms you and a release is required.
Leaving things unsaid fills your mind and deserves peace.
Embracing the emotional being that you are is essential.
Move through emotions even if it takes a while, be patient with yourself.
Block out external influences that don't feel good for you.
Express yourself freely and explore many forms of expression.

Journal entry, 4 December 2014: A life lesson from a fierce and determined spirit

Before my thirty-seventh birthday, I wrote this piece, and it was published in Sprout Online Magazine (now known as The Phoenix Soul) in December 2013. It has been one of the hardest and most vulnerable things I've ever written. After what I deemed to be a huge 2014 of healing, personal growth, empowerment and courage, I know I'm ready for this to be read by more people.

I won't lie to you. 2013 has been a challenging year for me. I have dwelled with dormant emotional trauma for over twenty years. I somehow thought I could leave it behind without repair but as I moved further along my path to discover my identity and purpose in life, it would remain dormant no longer. I woke up one morning last year after a poor night's sleep and typed out my story and how it made me feel and what mark it had left on my soul.

It had come to a point where I could not carry this baggage solo any longer. I've always found it difficult to ask for or accept help, even when it is offered. But this time I had to for my survival. I hit my 'ten', the panic button of overwhelm and defeat. I thought I was being swallowed up whole. My exterior crumbled as I opened my raw insides to the outside world and sought much-needed support from a professional and those closest to me. Later, I came to understand that I had other traumatic experiences to heal. So with fear, courage, and my loved ones and trusted friends alongside me, I began the process of healing. It led me to consider a lesson I've been trying to integrate: I have the power to get through anything, always.

This is just one piece of my life's puzzle. I have had three traumatic experiences to date at ages fourteen, twenty-two and twenty-three. I'm thirty-six now.

Confronting past trauma amid realising big dreams is such an overwhelming and conflicting set of circumstances to go through. I'm an artist and maker, and for about five months of this year, I painted and made nothing. I went through the motions in my professional day job. I put that brave smile on like a mask. I was shocked that my brain could carry this heavy weight for so long untreated. I minimised the toll it took on me for so long. I was scared at the thought of the long road to healing that not only was I emotionally blocked, but I was also creatively blocked too. I'd walk into my studio space, look around and walk back out and shut the door. It was stifling to not be able to use my creativity when I honestly needed an outlet.

I was angry that I allowed things to get to me. I was angry that I had these horrible experiences. But I learned that I had to be gentle on myself. I had to stop blaming and shaming myself. Enough of that had been done to me. I had done nothing wrong. I was a kid, a young woman. I was sexually and physically assaulted twice and experienced emotional abuse and manipulation on more than one occasion by an ex. He would belittle, shame, humiliate, manipulate and seek to control me and I ashamedly gave in because I had no self-worth and nothing in me to combat it. I was trapped and not equipped with the wisdom and knowledge of today to know that I didn't have to be there forever. I also didn't know how deeply it affected me until I dug deeper.

This year I have also faced my biggest fears—showing up, being vulnerable, marketing and talking to people at markets, showing my art in public, being scared that no one will like my work and sharing my life and inner thoughts on my blog. I did all of this while trying to heal, and when I look back, I'm a little bit amazed at how I got through the year. I'm a work in progress. There is still so much to heal, learn and confront, but I have the power, somehow, to get through it, always.

Connecting the dots

Journal entry, 12 October 2016

What once was, doesn't always remain. This is the impermanence of my art. This is the impermanence of life, the rhythm and cycle of birth, life and death.

I'm living not one life, but many within it. I feel like I am in a constant state of transformation, of evolution and while many of the changes are minute, they are contributing to my becoming.

I deepen my self-enquiry with more questions:

In what ways am I becoming more myself?

In what ways have I closed off or shut down because the vulnerable moments feel like more than I can take?

In what ways have I been lying to myself as though plaster can fill the cracks I no longer wish to see?

In what ways do I think I wiped the slate clean? How do remnants, history, stories, truths and deception still remain?

What is forced into hiding will not remain invisible. What is forced into silence will not remain silent.

Have you felt the rising? The rising of the silenced ones who will not be quiet any longer. Or the supporters, the ones who are saying 'speak up, declare your truth!'. The rising of the truth tellers who will share all their stories sans filters, censoring and edits.

The roars are audible and when they come, the silent ones will be the loudest. We, the quiet ones, will not conform. We will not do it another way. I will not do it the default 'right' way. My defiance to dismantle drives me. However, it also exhausts me, and I need to check my battery constantly.

Breaking open

Journal entry, 26 August 2014

Something that darkened my door for most of my life has popped up. I looked at the calendar and noted the date. I searched my sent box for emails to confirm my suspicion. Yes, two years. Two years since I reached out for the very first time in my three-plus decades of this life and asked for help. It was one of the hardest things I've ever had to do. I couldn't take any more of the same recurring nightmare, feelings of foreboding, keeping up and generally not feeling like I could move forward. The nightmares terrified me. When I was in that 'dream' scape all I could hear was static noise. I couldn't scream, I couldn't move, I was trapped. I had no voice, I was paralysed and there was no one there to help me. I do not know who or what was there in my nightmare, but the feelings paralleled a real-life situation in the level of fear, hopelessness and voicelessness. The nightmare crossed into reality, and I could hardly even move to wake myself up. I felt like I was completely awake wherever I was. My husband would wake me, after hearing muffled whimpering and I'd be in tears from frustration and fear. It took me a while to connect the dots and realise why these nightmares were happening. Two years ago, I had a gutful of it. I took the recurring nightmares as a sign that they would never end unless I asked for help. What was it? A traumatic experience from my early teens which had cast a dark shadow over a huge chunk of my life.

You don't realise until it happens to you, or someone you love, that not confronting a traumatic experience can grow and fester into something that just won't let you go. I was too young and naive to know any different.

I feel incredibly vulnerable. Like I'm uncovering something that needs to remain hidden away. Not out of shame or embarrassment, but because it takes a lot of trust and faith for me to open up, yet I am here breaking open.

One journey I made towards healing began two years ago and it hasn't been easy. In fact, it has often been a daily struggle. After I sought help in 2012, I made a little bit of peace with myself. I no longer blamed myself but I didn't keep up with talking to a professional because I thought I was done, and it was also hard to find a therapist who I felt really saw me. Turns out I wasn't done, there were other traumatic events to recover from, so 2013 was a challenging year professionally, personally and creatively. I required a huge dose of self-forgiveness to truly move forward.

I'm uncovering something that I thought needed to remain hidden away, not out of shame or embarrassment, but because it takes a lot of trust and faith for me to open up, yet I am here breaking open.

2022 Update: The nightmares are long gone, but not forgotten. I felt like I was moving through molasses as those nightmares had a strong hold over me and I experienced many recurrences of it. The nightmares described here stem from my story, Red Jumper, Blue Jeans.

Truthful thought

Journal entry, January 2017:
I let go of what does not serve
my highest good

This month has been a month of recharge, reclaiming, recalibration and rebuilding.

I've let go of so many things, stories, people and beliefs that I convinced myself I had to hold onto. I held myself back. I carried these old ways of being—and for what? A safety net of limitation? Responsibility to and for others? No more. I pulled back all of my energy in the spirit of sovereignty and in honour of my desire for 'fierce devotion' (these two words are tattooed on my left ribs so I can carry them with me always). I spoke up and out. I called people out. Enough with not feeling enough. Enough with being quiet and small.

I decided enough was enough when it came to making situations easier and more comfortable for others while I crashed and burned out. I said, 'enough bullshit' and turned my meter up higher to ensure I don't engage with who and where falsity, pandering, arse-kissing, highlights and shallowness simmer. I unsubscribed, unfollowed and unravelled everything. I don't need to be anyone but myself. I don't need other people's stuff. I could never follow it to the letter anyway. I have my own unique signature unfolding right now.

REFLECTION
QUESTIONS

- What will you let go of?
- When will enough be enough?
- When will you just walk your talk and traverse your own path instead of seeking the validation, attention and approval of others?

Sidenote: No one has walked that winding road. Allow stuff to fall away. If it's not for you, it won't stick around. No one knows you or your stories like you do. Tell your stories your way. You have a voice, and we all have a soapbox, so let's hear it, let's hear your wild truth.

5
Whole

'Honey, all you have to be by the of age 23 is yourself.'
—Troy in *Reality Bites* (1994)

I know WHO I am.
I will anchor into that MORE and EXPAND from that place.
These are the prophetic words that hit differently after
discovering I'm autistic and have ADHD.

What I wish I learned when I was younger

Wholeness and what it means to feel and be whole is different for everyone. Don't walk away because you think you're not worth it.

I've starved myself of love and affection many times in my life because I thought I wasn't worth it. I'm no longer ashamed to admit it because after years of playing small I realised that I deserved to give myself a fucking break and a chance at going for whatever it is that I want.

Now, let's make sure that this quote of mine is not taken out of context. Walk away if the love/job/career/relationship/friendship you want isn't giving you what you need.

The context and reason for this quote is to ask that you don't turn your back on your vision, your dreams or whatever is on your bucket list because you've come to the point in your personal development where you are facing worthiness challenges, or in my lived experience, worthlessness challenges.

If you are feeling resonance with this, I wish you KNEW how it feels in my body now to be embodied/connected to myself. To feel and be sovereign.

To know my truth.

To feel whole.

To feel deserving.

To feel worthy.

To feel truly loved on the inside and out.

To have found true love.

To be fully expressed.

To trust my voice.

To dissent from the lie.

My expression is my rebellion.

May yours become your rebellion.

I am becoming.

You are becoming.

Hello, I'm autistic

During the last phase of completing the manuscript of this book, I finally booked an appointment to see a doctor who I had been on the waitlist for since September 2021. Recommended by a friend after countless discussions about anxiety, ADHD and autism in relationships, I was on my way to hopefully receiving some answers and a way forward. I had an idea that ADHD would be a main topic of discussion, but it was not what came to bear.

By the time I saw the doctor for our first appointment, I was on the edge of major overwhelm and exhaustion. I wanted guidance and clarity, I needed to know. In the months before, I had to make some changes to my life and as I began implementing those it became very clear what I had been moving towards after my prophetic statement:

I know WHO I am. I will anchor into that MORE and EXPAND from that place.

What we discover may not be clear upon first receipt, but it can plant a seed or stoke a tiny spark to ignite, or bring forward a memory or series of memories where finally the picture is complete.

In my youth, being told 'I don't belong here' caused a massive ripple effect that has been a sleeping assassin throughout my whole life. I didn't want to belong then. I didn't feel like this world was for me, either. Without making promises to myself and not realising I couldn't be someone else if I tried, I was just myself. I heard about it often.

All my life I've felt on the outside, an outlier, awkward, too quiet, too shy, too direct, too blunt, too sensitive, too much, too many interests, too many obsessive habits and always at the edge but never quite fitting in anywhere. I created art and handmade jewellery in the early years of my business because I wanted to create beautiful things made with heart. As that progressed and I grew my skills to coaching and facilitation of online spaces over a six-year period, I knew that what I was created from was what I craved myself. I needed places I could just be me, while also being underdiagnosed, misdiagnosed and not receiving the treatment for the cause(s) and, as if by accident with no clear goal, I became someone who claimed their leadership. Experience and practise have been my best leaders. No formulas, lists or concentrated or watered-down goals of anybody else were ever going to do it for me in this life. My path has been one of wobbliness, transitions, crossroads, changes, life-altering choices and decisions that alter the paths of those travelling with me, my family. I've had to live it all, breathe it all and do it, make mistakes along the way, own my shit, shift, transform and refocus over and over again. It has been a lot for my mind computer, but I'm still here.

Reflecting on 2020, I thought I had figured out who I am and who the real me is. I had prophetic thoughts and visions about who that might be for years. A few more pieces of the puzzle dropped this year and in just a few weeks. There is a way forward, even if it looks like a series of big squiggly lines. We don't have to know it all and be it all in order to embrace purpose and the paths that are opening up for us.

We have choices, and one of those choices is to reclaim our minds and thoughts and get clear on what is learned behaviour and conditioning and what it is that we truly do believe. Cutting the bullshit lies from the truth is a daily battle. From the moment we open our eyes and look at a screen we are the target of sales. Some of that selling is directed at reducing us so we buy shit that won't work, but hey, they did it, so why can't I?

We are sold these 'simple' solutions that do not work for all of us because we possess different identities. I first heard the words 'empath' and 'highly sensitive person (HSP)' around 2013 to 2014. They seemed to simplify and give me some clarity over some of who I am, but this was not sustainable. How do you live with this advice?

All the heartache, unravelling and untangling of conditioning, belief, imposter syndrome and thinking I was just an empath and HSP when I went on to discover that I am much more complex and intense than that. I sought all types of healing and answers along the way and not always from the best places or qualified people early on.

So my doctor informed me that, yes, I have ADHD and hyper empathy. He asked me, 'Have you ever considered that you might be autistic?' to which I replied, 'No, the online assessments had me scoring shy of the minimum, so I set it aside.' Then it came, 'You are autistic.'

When the doctor told me, I cried. But I cried happy-ish tears because FINALLY I had answers, a plan moving forward, and maybe, just maybe, I would finally stop loathing myself. I think about how I do things in ways that are often vastly different to the 'norm', to the point where self-loathing and the worst self-talk have been the effects because I didn't know until I reached age forty-five.

Life is one big education, and it feels endless. I choose to and love to learn, and instead of more hobbies, interests and virtual rabbit holes to time warp into, I'm prioritising learning more about myself for a change.

I don't have to wear social masks to feel safe or 'normal' anymore—I didn't realise how good I got at acting and mirroring others. I also was unaware of just how taxing it was for me to change myself to be more acceptable to others. When it comes to social events, which unsurprisingly have greatly reduced over the past few years of living through a pandemic, I still do my pre-event prep of bath/shower, oils, breathing exercises and grounding because being at full charge or as close to full charge when there is a social event, is essential for me.

I observe and consume the world. It's my nature. I understand and think about human behaviour in ways I thought everybody did, but they don't. No wonder I'm often exhausted by people. I see right through people, and I see them with depth. This explains so much. No wonder I only have deep connections with a few people; this has been a pattern throughout my life! I don't have to be exhausted, anxious or afraid of every social situation, I can finally just get good at being me.

If it weren't for friends and clients who brought up neurodivergence with me, I might still be clueless about who I am. I'm super grateful to my loved ones, friends and clients who provided the safety and trust to explore and talk openly. I'm glad more and more of us are having conversations and holding space for each other.

I feel like I've unlocked a new level of myself. I know so many people who are late diagnosed like me or undiagnosed—self-diagnosis is valid too! We aren't all the same or have the same set of traits as other autistic and ADHD people.

Here's to learning more and being more of ourselves, supporting the autistic and ADHD people in our lives and busting the stereotypes, stigma and discrimination.

I am proudly autistic and ADHD.

I am continuing to let go of a heavy weight of emotions and feelings of not-enough-ness and instead choosing to embrace the 'wholeness' of me. It's not possible to receive the goodness, gems and gifts unless you accept the wholeness. I've spent the past few years readjusting my boundaries and it has taken a lot of work to let go of things, places and people to be more devoted to self-acceptance. With the support and information I have now, I have structured boundaries that serve me.

Learning that I'm autistic and have ADHD has been an enormous awakening. Spiritual exploration was the beginning of self-discovery, which started when I was thirteen, where I questioned belief systems and whether God even exists beyond human minds. I had been going to Sunday school at the church my parents were married in, even though neither were churchgoers. I was confirmed in the Church of England at thirteen. This was followed by an intense period during my teenage years wanting to know more about my beliefs. I went from reading metaphysical texts and books on witchcraft to learning the tarot to discover what interests me. From there, I moved to the question, 'Why do people believe what they believe?'.

For years I went down yet another rabbit hole reading about cults. A few years ago, I made another connection between those cult books and the cult dynamics employed in whitewashed spirituality. Spiritual exploration was not the be-all and end-all, because, deep breath, I'm a massive sceptic. I examine and question everything, including myself. I just wanted to figure things out. In unregulated industries like coaching and 'spiritual' thought leadership, we can go for years without proper care and diagnoses because buzzwords fill our feeds, relatable content convinces us that we are 'seen'; when some of those people at the top see us they just see dollar signs and luxury holidays. It's a smokescreen and can prevent us from discovering what we need to know about ourselves to live a full life. We can be led down the garden path because people on pedestals are self-titled as 'authorities' and 'experts'. I was led for a short time down that path and put people on pedestals because I didn't fully trust my own inner authority. I see right through fakery, I'm epically intuitive and I don't always voice and call it as I see it out of self-protection. If someone is a faker and false, I *know*.

You've maybe witnessed my direct approach to writing over the years, talking about and experiencing racism and being incredibly driven to shake people out of ignorance to become anti-oppressive in every way. I know and believe we can all do better. I'm not mean, uncaring, intimidating, unkind or apathetic. It's a simplification and a deflection of the people who write and say those words to me. I'm entirely the opposite, which is why I can and do the work I do. I own my shit. Do they own theirs?

I've been longing for belonging. I've jammed myself into spaces that didn't see, understand or embrace the full me. I tried practices, coaching, healing and techniques to help, heal and figure myself out, most of which didn't work. This was not my fault or the fault of the people who I chose (and paid) to guide and coach me. I didn't know or embrace all of myself, so how could they? Having space held for you to be witnessed and heard is awesome. It's a gift to be able to do this work as well. I require more. Coaching is wonderful but limited when we coaches aren't skilled in other areas like counselling, therapy, trauma awareness and beyond. We don't have to know it all or do it all either. We can, however, be aware and look to other support and avenues that complement our learning, education as a coach and to be coached, counselled and supported.

Belonging will look and feel different to each of us. What we need to feel as though we belong is different, too. What does belonging mean to you? If you are seeking belonging, what do you need and want from a space that holds, witnesses and truly embraces all of you?

Discovering that I am autistic has been the biggest revelation of my life. More than being bi, having ADHD, having PTSD (two diagnoses), racial trauma, anxiety, depression and panic attacks. I'm a late-diagnosed autistic human at age forty-five.

Some of my thoughts since finding out have been of grief, loss, wondering why the fuck nobody noticed sooner. What kind of a life would I have had if I had found out when younger, no wonder some relationships and friendships went the way they did and, ha! I knew I was different/awkward and exhausted after most social interactions, sometimes for days after, burned out by masking, mirroring, trying to read between all the lines of what people are not verbalising, but why? I could hyperfocus and mull over the disappointment, sadness, annoyance, frustration, feelings of grief for endless amounts of time, but what purpose would that serve me? I am paying attention to those and allowing time and space to process as I go. No denial of my emotions or feelings, just not letting them influence my days.

This is one thing I know: there's time. I have time. There's time for me at age forty-five to embrace all of me for the rest of my life, however long or short that is, and build a life knowing more about myself and how I show up in the world, and do so being all of me.

I believe that through my writing I share a lot of who I am and how I navigate life. I don't filter or censor my self-expression. I've been writing online for ten years since I began blogging. I realise I have not hidden, coddled or masked my words in any way. I often write as I'm thinking, and you basically get the live stream of my thoughts through my words. I don't edit much these days. How I write is how I think (but with a dozen more tangents and questions) and I've oscillated from mulling over writing for days and weeks before hitting post and publish to banging out some words within minutes. I speak plainly and some would say, bluntly. I say what I want to say when writing about issues: anti-racism, anti-oppression and inclusion, and for the people I care most about—gender diverse and racialised people—over the past five years.

Doing this work has been my contribution, a huge investment of my time, energy, labour, fierce research and self-taught learning skills. It has been an outpouring of love, a real passion for helping others to expand their views of the world, to untangle from every layer of oppressive bullshit and to prioritise heart over harm in every moment. I'm not a six- or seven-figure entrepreneur, and while that would be nice and make life so much easier (and more multiple six- or seven-figure entrepreneurs *should* be working with me), it's not high on my list of goals. I just want to be comfortable, not worry and stress about income and be able to afford to live. I've spent thousands of hours creating free and low-dollar content. People still baulked. I low-balled myself on my rates for most of the past few years and, fuck, it has been so hard to find clients and students to work with me! I know what I need to be paid for now and I've updated everything and removed some services. I have also over-created these past four years. A handful of the things I've created have not worked out. Overall, I felt like I failed a lot. Some parts of me still do.

You don't get this honest, blunt and chaotically overworked and over-energised to burned out and frozen, or caring and compassionate to the point of emotional pain and anguish for nothing! I don't subscribe to the belief that 'everything happens for a reason'. That's reductive and gross. History has shown us plenty that has happened that hasn't made sense. Privilege, power and control are utilised for the sole benefit of the players who have it all and it's lorded over many of us.

Autistic life

I am an autistic human with ADHD and hyper empathy. I'm writing about my own experiences even though it is very early days in comprehending this newfound information. At the time of writing this, it has been two months since the revelation with my doctor. I'm still processing and will likely continue to process this information for the foreseeable future.

I wonder what my life would have been like had I learned this information much sooner than age forty-five. I'm sceptical it would have even been discovered or diagnosed given the assumptions of neurotypical and allistic (non-autistic) people around what autism is, who has it and how it presents in each autistic individual. Our traits and experiences, while similar, are unique to each of us. Upon learning more about how these three conditions overlap and interrelate with each other, I'm learning just how complex and confusing my life has been and how I've worn various masks to cope, mirroring what is acceptable and normal, while also not conforming and being resistant to conformity. It makes me sad knowing that it's not just me. Many people go through life without knowing or never finding out. No wonder I have felt so alone throughout my entire life even when surrounded by loved ones. I have never wished I was normal. I like being different in the various ways that I am.

I remember my ma taking me to the doctor when I was in grade 5 or 6 because she thought I had a hearing problem when I was just so hyper-focused on whatever I was doing that I wouldn't stop what I was doing to respond to her. My grade 6 teacher wrote a poem for the class with every line about each class member. Mine was 'Sharyn, the quiet achiever'. That's me or was back then: quiet and getting things done.

Today, I'm much the same but with a hefty serving of giving no fucks and speaking up so I can get things done. Some things don't change.

If I'm to analyse myself now and who I thought I was before I knew, there is grief in my heart for the girl who grew up to be me. There is grief for young adult me trying to navigate the world feeling like I'm here, but I don't 'fit' or have the same operating system as those around me. I now know being autistic has been the root of many friendships in my life ending, including relationships. It has meant being deemed weird and having 'strange' ideas about things and often being misinterpreted over and over. Facts don't cause people to change their ideas or beliefs. Facts can seem confrontational to people who want fluff and to bubble wrap every piece of communication. For me, adding fluff instead of just being my direct and blunt self is an energy sucker. I will never forget to be kind though.

I've fallen into the trap of believing that the problem is me, bearing the weight of blame and shame for things not working out, or that my communication was too direct or that I was too emotional and sensitive. Untangling myself from this and many other beliefs will be a journey of unravelling for the rest of my life.

I told people closest to me first and, oddly enough, many of my friends and clients are neurodivergent, too. It was actually a couple of friends and clients who got me thinking early last year that I could be neurodivergent, too. These open and caring conversations have made the new self-awareness easier. I went public when I learned I was autistic because silence is painful, and we as autistic people need to know that there are other people like us, too. I wrote about it for the autistic and neurodivergent people in my online community.

As I limit my social interactions and have developed strong boundaries over the past four years, I'm yet to experience the awful, 'you don't look autistic', and similar comments that I've read so many autistic people receive. If I'm logical about it, my thought process about this would be, *what the hell do they know, really?* Excuse me, but your ableism is showing. There isn't one defined appearance of what autism looks like. Why say something that could be hurtful and harmful when someone is open enough to trust you to tell you this about themselves? Do we say this to people who receive other diagnoses that aren't visible? I put it down to my depth of thought, as I know no other way than to really plumb the depths. I'm always thinking about the impact of my words, and I do everything possible to make sure I don't harm anyone.

There are people in my life who I still haven't told. It's not an easy conversation to start when it feels like a coming-out announcement. I've been there and did that in 2018 when I came out as bisexual. I'm already bracing myself for what may come when and if these people and others read this book. I've already heard the comment, 'it doesn't change anything', and to those people or anyone who might say those words to someone someday, this is what I have to say in advocating and speaking up for myself: knowing changes everything.

Imagine living your whole life and missing the memo on a significant part of yourself, one that would affect your entire life without it. I should've been born with a user manual. Knowing I'm autistic changes not only how I feel about myself, but also how I feel about people I've crossed paths with when I couldn't have done anything differently because I wasn't equipped. As an autistic person, it is not my job to make others feel good about it. I'm happy to be autistic, elated even, because it has been a stunning revelation, bigger than anything else I've learned about myself and other diagnoses I've had like PTSD (twice), anxiety and a panic disorder.

How many of you will get to your forties and beyond and do a full-scope reflection of your life to make sense of it and digest all the pieces and parts you've come to learn about yourself? Writing this book and writing online as I have done since 2012 has enabled that entire life reflection. I'm glad I had the guts to start a blog and become published online and in zines over the years, and to keep writing in the face of trolls, hate, sealioning and seemingly endless misunderstanding online when I expanded my writing and created resources to include anti-racism and anti-oppression in 2017.

I'm thankful for people in the public eye like Hannah Gadsby for sharing her experiences as an autistic person, and for every comment and personal story shared by autistic people in Facebook groups, and for every conversation I've had with neurodivergent clients and friends. It's through these conversations and communities that I've felt a higher sense of belonging.

I have never felt like I fitted in or belonged anywhere, with the exception of the gothic subculture that I became a part of shortly before my eighteenth birthday. The dancefloor at goth nightclubs was my church in my early adulthood and onwards, because I still love to dance the way I feel when the rare opportunity presents itself. While writing this book, my BFF and I reminisced over our younger years and despite all the turbulent times of youth and being part of a scene, those times with my friends on the dancefloor live on. My BFF and I spoke about how good those years together were. Over the past few years, I've scheduled trips back to Sydney to see my parents and BFF to coincide with anniversaries of the clubs we used to go to almost thirty years ago. Seeing old faces from decades before still moving on the dancefloor in what I'd describe as group euphoria. The faces, moves, bodies and sweat coming together to dance to the anthems of our youth.

Last year, we went along to the thirtieth anniversary of a club night called Sanctuary. In the 90s the original club closed but returned in the form of various events. We had some amazing nights back then. Returning was like being twenty again, dancing next to my BFF. Still having the stamina for occasional late nights and dancing with the aftermath of smoke machine-scented hair and very sore feet shows that twenty-year-old me is alive and well. I'm still a goth at heart even if my wardrobe and makeup is not as goth as it once was. I still have the music and happy memories. The social challenges and relationship spirals experienced during those years were a training ground.

Looking back, I first noticed what I learned to be meltdowns in my early relationships. I often wonder if neurotypical people were just trying to find fault with me or the way I react and respond emotionally to all matters as a way of deflecting responsibility for their part.

I see the paradox in myself as a formerly 'shy' and introverted person who doesn't back down and isn't afraid of confrontation and difficult conversations. I've been having difficult conversations for my whole life; it's not a new or recent thing. Those difficult conversations started in my primary school playground as teasing that developed into racial bullying, body shaming and sexism in high school, working with apathetic, small-minded and ignorant people in the workplace and receiving threats and hateful, horrid comments and emails in response to my anti-racism, anti-oppression and inclusion writing online.

As I begin to chisel these masks off, I am feeling an increasing sense of peace within, love for myself that I never had and self-acceptance, finally. I belong to me and that's what matters. I'm holding myself with kindness instead of just trying to hold myself together. It has been a long haul getting here. Getting these words down on the page is hugely intense and I've been crying as I type this because of how emotionally overwhelming it is. The load I've carried all this time has been beyond my comprehension—how did I survive like this for so long?

I'm focused on the paths and choices ahead and looking forward to embracing myself fully. To appreciate and value all that's peculiar and weird about me and deepening self-acceptance because it is the combination of my unique qualities, experiences, how big my heart is, how much I care, how deep feeling I am and how I choose to do things, and the way my mind operates, that make me special. I'm fulfilling my potential in various ways. With every limit or fear that I come across, I'm a formidable opponent. Patti Smith wrote in *Just Kids*, 'I would go as far as I could and hit a wall, my own imagined limitations. And then I met a fellow who gave me his secret, and it was pretty simple. When you hit a wall, just kick it in.'

Autistic and ADHD

I was looking for photos on my phone and came across a black and white selfie of me wearing my unicorn hooded blanket. Who I am has been here all along. This part of the chapter comes late in the writing process. Weeks away from the manuscript deadline. We are moving house in four weeks—address unknown—I started a new job two weeks ago, my daughter is about to turn sixteen and I've just about reached boiling point and then a new knowledge hits. I mean HITS.

The ADHD roasted burnt plum potion

I have an inside joke I want to let you in on. Time warps are real. Ask any person with ADHD.

I've tried everything from timers to carrying around kitchen utensils to remind myself that I have something on the stove or in the oven.

With a mind computer that is always switched ON with the dial turned right up, it takes little effort to find a dozen things to immerse myself in when I'm supposed to be keeping an eye on my plums.

REFLECTION QUESTIONS

- If you resonate with neurodivergence, are autistic and/or have ADHD that is diagnosed/self-diagnosed/suspected, what do you want to learn about yourself?
- How do you want to support yourself?
- Where can you seek reliable and helpful guidance?
- Celebrate your differences: what makes you so wonderfully, brilliantly and uniquely, you?
- Hot tip: consider also joining some online neurodivergent chats for connection, advice and camaraderie (my favourites are on Twitter).
- What do you wish you knew when you were younger?
- In what ways can you resource and support yourself now with the lessons you've discovered?
- What actions could you take to challenge your fears?
- What freedom will overcoming your fears give you?

- Where can you receive support, care and compassion to become the fullest version of you?
- Explore wholeness. How do you define it for yourself?
- What makes you feel whole?
- How can you internally resource yourself to wholeness?
- What resources, support, guidance and people do you need in your corner?

Activating you

You are divine.
You are beloved.
You deserve respect, love, trust and boundaries.
You are a radiant beam of light.
You are cosmic dust.
You are your own home.
Your body is your sacred temple
to be honoured, loved and revered.
Treat it kindly, showing others how to do the same.
You deserve this time for yourself, to be in all your magic
to be present, feeling every breath to your core, to feel every sinew,
muscle and bone in your body.
You allow your intuition to lead.

6
Mother

'my mother
is pure radiance.

she is the sun
i can touch
and kiss

and hold
without
getting burnt.'
—Sanober Khan

Becoming a mother changed everything for me. The day I discovered that I was pregnant, my husband, Ryan was away motor racing for the weekend. I had noticed in the week prior that the pain relief I was taking for daily headaches was not helping. It was only after a week of this that I suspected that my period was late, but at that time I wasn't really tracking my cycle particularly well. I went to the chemist and purchased a pregnancy test and went home. I took the test, and as I saw the result, I looked up and saw my face in the mirror and felt a joy unlike any other. We were going to have a baby. I phoned Ryan shortly after on that day in September to share the news. That Sunday it was Father's Day, which made the news all the more special for us both.

I had a relatively easy pregnancy aside from the stretched ligaments around my coccyx. I had to sit on an exercise ball at work because the pain I felt when I sat in an office chair was awful.

My parents and my in-laws were thrilled with our news. This would be the first and only grandchild for my parents and the second out of three for my in-laws.

When I shared the baby news with my work friend Sonya, she about crash-tackled me right on the street. It was wonderful to share this news with someone who was so happy for us. This news came just five months after we got married.

We wanted a surprise, so we didn't 'find out what we were having'. To us, it didn't matter, so long as we had a healthy baby. I never gave much thought to gender back then. Today, I'm a party pooper when it comes to gender reveal parties—not that I've ever been invited to one or personally know anyone who has had one. If we make ourselves aware and expand our range of thinking, we can know so much more about the *spectrum* of gender today. As I've paraphrased elsewhere in this book, gender binary is bullshit. We can broaden our understanding, change our thinking and be better at allowing and accepting people who self-identify their gender, because it is more than just biology or our opinion. Lives are at stake.

As the big day approached, we planned and organised, made the necessary purchases, and I had regular appointments with my obstetrician. We were fortunate to have arranged a family private health insurance plan a while before, so we were partially covered financially. One of the things that brought us peace of mind was that my employer provided maternity leave benefits. You could receive three months at full pay or six months at half pay and take up to twelve months off. This was back in 2006 sometime before more employers made this a part of company policy. In the end, I took eight months off and returned to work three days a week. Our daughter was in childcare one day a week and my parents would look after her on the other day.

The obstetrician who I had seen for many months before was away on holiday. He failed to tell me this until I asked a couple of months before the birth.

Early on the morning of 28 April 2006, I woke up completely alert. Something was happening and it felt as though someone was arriving right on time. I began to have contractions. The pain was similar to menstrual cramps. My menstrual cramps were more on the severe side and while this was really uncomfortable, it wasn't a 'bad' pain. It was going to be a very special day! I called the hospital and they advised me to stay home as my water had not broken yet. I shooed Ryan off to work a few hours later. The pain intensified after that, and I found myself on all fours alternating between the bath and the loungeroom floor to breathe through the contractions. I called the hospital another few times with an update. My water still hadn't broken so they told me to stay put.

As the pain grew more intense and the contractions were closer together, I phoned Ryan and asked him to come home. Within a half hour of his arrival, I was on the phone again to the hospital, waters still unbroken, and I said I was coming to the hospital now and that was it. Ryan drove us to Randwick and the contractions were full on. When we arrived at the hospital car park and I got out of the car, contractions were coming closer together. I propped myself up against a pillar, hands first, as another contraction took hold. Ryan waved at passers-by as they showed concern. Once inside the hospital, they checked me over. I was 8cm dilated. This was at about 11 a.m.. I took some gas and tried unsuccessfully to not crush Ryan's hand as labour was well underway.

As the hours passed, I grew impatient. I am one of those people who, if you give me a ballpark amount of time, I can deal. This male obstetrician whom I had only met just a couple of weeks before kept telling me to calm down as I continued to ask, 'how much longer?' and 'is there time for some pain relief?'. Looking back, I'm pretty annoyed at the situation, There I was giving birth and he couldn't answer my questions? I was a bit too busy to articulate my reasons for insisting. There was a bit of trouble getting our daughter out and I unfortunately ended up with a third-degree tear and an episiotomy. Yay, stitches in my nether regions. On the plus side, the nurse assisting with delivery had a Northern Irish accent which I found very soothing.

Then, she was here, our girl. Behind her, my waters gushed out. Our healthy 3.73kg baby covered in white goo had blocked my waters. We stayed in the hospital for a couple of days before we went home. Life changed forever. I never knew how this precious baby would teach me how to mother myself in ways I didn't deem myself worthy.

The first few weeks were hard, and I was hard on myself. We were sleep deprived, but our daughter was a pretty good sleeper, doing four-plus-hour stints early on. I had little milk and supplemented with formula before my supply dried up after a few weeks. A visit with a paediatrician a few months later brought the words I needed to hear. The breast milk I was able to provide was beneficial. I had been beating myself up because I had read all the paraphernalia on breastfeeding and unfortunately took the shaming aspects with me and the phrase 'breast is best'. I felt like a failure because I couldn't provide more breastmilk. That feeling didn't go away for quite some time and I ended up internalising the shame more and more, and as my hormones went haywire, my mood dimmed.

I went to our local mothers' group for a little while. We rented in a very affluent area at the time, and I felt like I had nothing in common with these women. I was never very good at small talk or surface-level conversations, so I eventually left the group and, in doing so, I isolated myself.

The news came shortly after our daughter was born that I had an abnormal pap smear result, CIN 3 as a result of HPV which I had caught from a previous partner some years before. The doctor recommended LEEP to remove the spot from my cervix. I was booked in for October. Three weeks before, I caught chicken pox. I had never had chicken pox, mumps, measles or anything and I got really sick for a couple of weeks. The first few days as the spots spread from my stomach to everywhere including my scalp, I was so fatigued. I'd get out of bed to go to the toilet, and then I had to go back to bed. I was so exhausted. My ma came to stay to help take care of Sahra when Ryan was at work.

After I started to feel better, more isolated behaviour occurred. I felt so self-conscious of my spots that I didn't go out during the day. Ryan would come home from work and we'd go for evening walks. My mood was really low and I felt so confused by it. I was highly emotional and had regular meltdowns where I couldn't even remember what I was saying after they happened. Ryan urged me to get some help, but I was in denial and so overwhelmed I couldn't think straight.

Soon after I recovered from chicken pox, I went in for my day surgery. It was recommended that I didn't carry Sahra for a few days while I recovered. I recall this being really hard to deal with at the time. I was feeling sad a lot even though I had this beautiful baby I was raising. Despite my low mood and depressive feelings within and towards myself, I never lost my love or connection to her.

My denial about needing help continued for months after I returned to work. I found a suitable local GP and they diagnosed me with postnatal depression and Vitamin D deficiency. She recommended I speak with a psychologist, but I wasn't ready for that. Eventually, I improved and moved on with life. We had this beautiful, chubby, little person to raise. I look back at those early days of motherhood and remember them fondly, despite my personal struggles.

Our daughter is sixteen years old now. Parenting has been quite a ride and I'm proud to say that we are raising a sassy and independent young person.

Coming home to myself

This little human that I birthed is growing into an inquisitive, deeply caring, independent and assertive person. From the parquetry floor of our apartment where she took her first steps after several months of running about on her knees. To the sandy coloured lounge we would curl up on for stories, *In the Night Garden* and *The Wiggles*, in which she liberally applied MAC Viva Glam lipstick to not only herself but to the lounge as well while I was in the bathroom (swiftly removed, no stains). To her extreme love of pistachios and wasabi peas. Twinning. Her facial expressions and piercing glare almost put me to shame. I am so proud of that. Also, her eyebrows. All of which I get to see every single day (especially the glare), mainly because when words pour out of my mouth she tells me I'm weird and not funny. She's direct, honest and forthright.

She has taught me so much about life by her very existence and, somehow, I knew she would from the first time I saw her in a dream in my early twenties, the full cheeks and big brown eyes framed by short dark brown hair. That's not to put the weight of my world on her shoulders, not at all. It's as full as I can put into words, a personal acknowledgement that it truly is a privilege to love, nourish and support the thriving of another human being, and I hope that I've done all I can to ensure she grabs the world with both hands, forges her path and lives the life she dreams and hopes for. I hope I've shown her by trial, fire and transformation that I have explored the world, turned my hand to many arts and crafts, read and collected many books and stickers, beaten silver into jewels, been an employee with a side gig to self-employed. By struggling and treading water but always rising, I've created an example of what she might want for the breadth of her life.

It's no small thing to say that someone changed my life, and I am the willing accomplice and executor. She has. There are many ways that I could tell you, but it would be easier for me to show you through my stories, timeline, passions, path, choices, decisions, creativity, creation, innovation, challenges, obstacles and triumphs and great memories along the way.

She has also been a very big part of my heart throughout my entire online experience. Gutsy Girl was created because of our daughter. Sure, I was called gutsy in high school, but that is a mere detail alongside why I had the courage to start a blog, begin Gutsy Girl, have it morph into circles and coaching and be invited to live speaking events and teaching opportunities. Our two hearts built the courage I inevitably required to take the leap, begin, try, persevere, fumble, rumble all while staying humble, and not giving up on what I believe is true, kind, right and just.

As she has grown there have been some challenges, obstacles and bullying that she has faced, however, those stories are her own and not for me to share.

I began Gutsy Girl when our daughter was in grade 1. This was initially as a writing outlet for my art journal explorations and musings about spirituality and creativity, before I evolved it to workshops and circles after a missed opportunity to attend a workshop caused me to create and launch my own. My workshop was Creative Fire, covering courageous conversations, breathwork, journaling, art making and mapping. I followed this with monthly moon circles which I ran for a few years before taking my circle online and teaching circle leadership facilitation. I had my first public speaking opportunity in 2017 and wanted more. I spoke with my coach at the time, Jade McKenzie, about wanting to create an amazing event. It took me a couple of years to come back to the idea after my redundancy in 2018.

Another version of me birthed soon after my redundancy and eight years of work. I was going to try self-employment. I was excited, motivated, inspired and I had lots of ideas, many of which I attempted to execute all at once. I was on this constant whirligig of fun, working, family life, creating, writing, learning, and coaching for too long without taking the foot off the accelerator. Boom. I burned out. I began suffering from chronic migraines in August 2020, the year the world opened its sleepy old eyes to racial justice, Black Lives Matter and more police brutality for several weeks before returning to business as usual in the COVID-19 pandemic world. The world was at home, many comfortable and safe with time and vitriol ready to burn some toxicity on social media and harm others, instead of 'taking a good look in the mirror' and asking themselves, 'What the FUCK are YOU going to do to make a difference?'.

I was fired up and fuelled up after re-educating myself and broadening my lens on the world, social change, community and racial justice. I was compelled to write about it and I did. I started my Patreon community in 2017 before moving to ko-fi in 2021. I have written extensively on personal storytelling, racial awareness, anti-racism, anti-oppression, gender inclusivity, representation, equity and inclusion ever since. First at a rabid and rapid pace that, today, I need a nap at the thought of. I was like this for years. I went full-time self-employed #GirlBoss in mid-2018. No, really, but without the #GirlBoss. My writing streak has hardly stopped since then. I spent countless hours creating writing content on Instagram, for my Patreon community, in the creation and development of Gutsy Leadership, Formidable Voices, Unpack Your Privilege, Witchuition and Inclusive Coach.

I missed meals. Self-care took a backseat, aside from baths and massage. I was offering a lot and coaching and teaching a lot of people, but I didn't have spaces and communities where I could be there receiving. I came late to this realisation near the end of 2020, and set about figuring out what it was that I wanted to achieve and re-engineer it so I could formulate a plan. It made me really sad to realise that my outputs were always 110 percent but I was lucky to be in double digits for myself. My cup was running on empty, and my physical symptoms were painful, prolonged and awful. I experienced a lot of bodily pain and my digestive system was malfunctioning. It took me a year to strengthen my boundaries to make the essential changes. I needed to make some changes, and fast. I pared back on my almost daily Instagram posting, realising it was a massive drain of my energy, output and labour. It took me much longer to recognise that the physical symptoms were due to the pace and pressure I had put upon myself. I had to stop.

Here was another recurring lesson: everything will come to a grinding halt if you do not take care of yourself. I would speak to my husband, and he has always been great for a reality check and directness when it comes to me: 'Don't you think you deserve to be happy?'. Snapping my thoughts back to logic and facts, which, as it turns out, serve a greater purpose to me than my anxiety mind computer and its constant spinning wheel. I spent close to five years getting direct with the facts and logic and straight to the point and the heart of matters. It was widely appreciated but it was also wild at how nasty people were or became because they didn't like my communication style and approach, and would tone-police, correct and try to shame me for what I dared to write. I received nasty DMs and comments, anything from death threats and cruelty to my family and our dogs to, basically, bitches being white and me being perceived as intimidating, mean and angry. The latter is true but 'intimidating and mean'? Anger is a healthy emotion and I had decades of internalised rage, pain and trauma that I had the lid on for most of my life, and she was gonna blow. I knew the purpose of these messages and it is a sad reality for many of us; the purpose is to silence us. These people want us to stop talking, to stop causing them to think and feel, or to be uncomfortable, to erase us, to prevent our voices from being heard. However, I am still writing and have been saying what needs to be said for five years now, mostly non-stop. I haven't gone away. I haven't been quiet. I've seasoned my voice. Have you seasoned your chicken?

Is it ironic that the grade 6 quiet achiever would turn out like this? It's like that line from *Network*, 'I'm as mad as hell and I'm not going to take it anymore!' paired with Heart's 'Barracuda' and Rage Against The Machine's 'Wake Up', and you'll have created the perfect little recipe for me to write some 6 million words up until now.

Mothering me

Since 2006, I have spent the years mothering me. I didn't take care of myself or my heart particularly well for a very long time. I believed the lies and thought I was unworthy and didn't deserve much. I stayed when I should have left. I left when I should have said something. For every door I've opened, there are ones still ajar that I'm now willing to close. My life since I was twenty-six has been the best part. That's a lot of years and a lot of good times. They were also some of my most tumultuous and anguished years, exploring my pain and trauma, picking apart my behaviours and beliefs, expanding my thinking and learning while gratefully being in love, loving and loved. I can ascribe no responsibility to any one person for being where I am now. It was a team effort. Yes, the team includes the naysayers, trolls, saboteurs, foes and faux friends, too.

My husband showed me a mirror to myself that I had not seen, embraced or reflected on. Sometimes the medicine we need is our own and having someone be that person to give it to you is a wonderful privilege. I feel so grounded in myself now, even though I'm learning about big aspects of myself in general, and through writing this book.

The mothership journey to who I'm here to be

Let my defining moment in life not be one of trauma and pain but one of great joy that will provide more learning, love and happiness than I could ever imagine.

I have had some great joys in life. I'm fortunate to have had them. I'm fortunate to have people in my life that I love to the core. When I consider the list of moments and experiences that changed me, I don't want the first things that come to mind to be the ones that broke me, the ones where I was physically, sexually, emotionally and psychologically hurt by human beings that cared only for themselves and what they wanted. Those moments do not define who I am, those people do not get to live on the life raft I built myself. Life experiences can change us, but we are always more than what happened to us.

What I wish my younger self knew is: don't settle for less than what you deserve. Don't let other people's insecurities colour your self-worth or dim your light. Do right by you. It's important that your life involves upping your self-worth, developing and trusting your gut instinct and transforming yourself, not for the benefit of others, but to live the life you are meant to lead. If a relationship is not giving you a full-bodied YES, you are being mistreated, put down and disrespected. This is a sign that it's time to go.

My greatest joys required patience and trust to arrive. My greatest joys have been the ultimate surprises, too. Meeting my future husband at age twenty-five. That was a great joy. The day we got married. Another great joy. The day we found out I was pregnant. Great joy. The day our daughter was born. The greatest joy. Motherhood has brought more joy, wisdom, love and learning than I could ever have expected from life.

Of all the things I've had to learn in life, raising gutsy girls tops the list. I'm not just a mother to a child. There is more to my identity than that. Though often as women, society defines us by whether or not we have birthed a new life into this world. Finding myself has been hard, and while motherhood and identity are inextricably linked for me personally, I don't believe that women should be defined by whether they become mothers or not. We can reclaim ourselves. We get to choose. We know who we truly are, deep down. I believe we are the only ones that can define ourselves. And sometimes, there are too many words to list for all that we are, all that we were and all that we might become.

I am a mother.

I am an artist and I am an earthshaker and beyond that, I am formidable and sovereign.

I am a mother to myself.

REFLECTION
QUESTIONS

- If you are a mother, document and write your memories, stories and experiences.
- Unpack what being mothered / not being mothered has meant for you and seek support as needed.
- What does being mothered involve for you?
- How can you reimagine being mothered by taking the reins yourself?
- Who is involved in your motherhood and/or mothering self-journey?
- Learning to mother yourself is an act of self-love and acceptance. What actions can you take towards mothering yourself?

7
Becoming Gutsy

'I've been absolutely terrified every moment of my life—and I've never let it keep me from doing a single thing I wanted to do.'
—Georgia O'Keeffe

If you're hoping for a straight road, a cohesive, comprehensive and consistent story written in a single voice or frame of mind, disappointment awaits. I wrote half the content of this book over a period of years while I was living through and documenting those moments. The other half of the book was written post-pandemic after a long period of deep self-reflection, adjustment, letting go and rebirth. Within these pages are the many selves of my existence, all of whom are here today in the flesh. I'm not talking about personalities or personas; I'm talking about the many layers and traits that make up who I am that are enlisted at any one point in time to deal with life stuff. I am a forever student of the rollercoaster of life; my formal training and qualifications are spottier than a Dalmatian.

I involve myself in what interests me, I stumbled my way into love, I feel everything so very deeply that it hurts, or it gives me a huge sense of euphoria that I can't really explain.

As I've written this book, I've breached my share of crossroads, grown away from friendships as my special interests and passions have expanded and come to a place of peace that now I've felt, it's a mood away. I'm learning that as I've lived the life I'm living, I've cultivated chameleon-like qualities. It's probably a familiar story for us neurodiverse, racialised and melanated people. The dress rehearsals, the costume changes, the different voices and masks required to exist. I have tried in my own way to bring clarity, completion and compassion to my story. It's time. There's a lot of talk about forgiveness when trauma is a part of a person's story. In mine, I'm the person who has needed forgiveness and grace. I wished I learned that sooner but now I know, everything changes, everything can be different, and I can continue to move forward, closing the doors on my personal stories in this book.

Becoming curious

We live in an age where misinformation abounds, where people are complicit in upholding systems of oppression and information is weaponised, and where people don't check their facts when they are communicating out in the world because they have an agenda that aims to serve only them.

This is why it is so important to become a truth seeker and *become curious.*

For some of us, that's deeply embedded into who we are from a very young age.

Finding truth is a journey of discovery, one that you come across from many different angles.

Becoming a truth seeker, to me, is about finding out not only the truth of any given matter or topic, particularly that of oppression, but also finding my truth within.

I believe we can start at either point.

But for me, I had to find the truth within myself to determine what I believed or followed or was informed by the truth out there.

Intuition is my compass

It took me a long time to trust that my intuition is my guide, to trust myself. In 2014, I discovered that my intuition and empath traits are a gift. They do not fail me. I look back and see how I failed myself by taking on what others think and feel about how they think I should think and feel. What I can tell you is, you must trust yourself first. Be your own guide, carve your own path.

Intuition, natural instinct, gut feeling, inner guide, second sight, sixth sense, inner truth, whatever you call it you know it simply by feel. Your intuition knows no words, it simply responds with a shiver on your skin, tension in your body, wave in your stomach, heaviness in your heart area, hair raising on your arms or a tear in your eye. Feel it and always know it to be true.

You can't fight your feelings, though you may try. Others may tell you that how you feel or what you are feeling is wrong. What do they know? They simply don't. Your intuition doesn't lie. People do.

Think about the moment you hear a song on the radio that takes you back to another time in your life, whether it was good or bad. Feel it.

- When I watch someone sing with such passion or sorrow, I get prickles on my skin and quite often, tears will fall. These are my natural responses to beauty.
- When I am disappointed or feel like I've failed, I feel heaviness in my chest, a sinking feeling in my stomach and my head aches.
- When I dance, I feel free, I feel joy and I feel limitless. I am totally present in that moment, and I never want it to end.
- When I paint, I am free, not conforming to any rules or guidelines. I am immersed right into it. I'm free from my thoughts and worries.
- When I create or write, I feel excited, invigorated, ALIVE, the words or ideas cannot be contained. This is the moment when the glass is overflowing and spilling

everywhere.

- When I make jewellery, it's a meditative process. I feel like an alchemist, transforming and melding magic with metal.
- When I was cut down by a friend in a serious time of need, I felt like someone had slapped my face. I felt the sting of her words on my face.
- When I meet someone and I'm uneasy or can't pinpoint why, I take note and am cautious. My intuition is trusted here.
- When I feel love and am loving, I feel like it's a day at the beach, fresh salty ocean air, the sunshine warm like a big hug given and received.
- When I feel grounded and balanced, I feel like it's a walk along the creek, rock hopping or simply sitting, sensing all the nature sounds, noticing the dappled light through the trees, clinging to the trees as we walk and weave our way through, the sounds of rushing water and the reflection of the sky on the water surface.

Feel all your feelings. The hard and painful ones are the worst but know what they feel like. It's confronting, you will resist but you need to know for sure. Have faith in your intuition, always.

REFLECTION
QUESTIONS

- What are you curious about?
- What would you like to learn more about?
- What would you like to integrate into your life right now?
- Are you a sensitive and sensory human? What does that look like for you?

- What can you do to support, nourish and honour your capacity and energy?
- Are you intuitive?
- Do you trust your intuition?
- In what ways can you notice and develop it more?

8
Artist

Teachers come in many forms, and none are to be discounted or underestimated. I claimed the title of artist because of my daughter. When I began Gutsy Girl, she had just turned six years old.

She would tell her friends that I was an artist. I realised that it wasn't something I had claimed for myself. It caused me discomfort just like every other title and role I've reluctantly claimed in my life. There has, for a long time, been this sense of not being enough, not being worthy and not feeling qualified enough even after a decade or more of experience.

Thanks to the combination of my daughter's beautiful wisdom at such a young age, the coaching, teaching and guidance of people including Staci Jordan Shelton, Desiree Adaway, Ericka Hines, McKensie Mack, Nisha Moodley and Sora Schilling, I overcame, or probably more accurately, began practising enough-ness, worthiness and finally believing that I had stories worth telling. Art provided stimuli and sensory experience in a different way to music. The art of Salvador Dali, René Magritte, Yayoi Kusama, Vincent van Gogh and Gustav Klimt, alongside modern and indie artists and makers of all kinds, have inspired me with their artistry and that breath of life only art and music can provide. Art enlivens. Art saved me in sensation and practice. Mastery? For me, nope. I love to experiment and play and do and practices that brings joy. Through art, circles, coaching, mentoring, teaching and, of course, writing. At the heart, no matter what I do for work, I am an artist.

An awakening

My first ever exhibition was in 2014. I pushed myself for months while confronting a long-standing past trauma condition and treating it properly for the first time. It was almost too much to deal with. I suffered many creative blocks that lasted for weeks at a time throughout the majority of 2013. I was highly sensitive, and my boundaries were down, so the words of other people—particularly people who didn't know me well enough—felt harsh or teasing and hurtful.

Resistance and procrastination reigned, and I inadvertently allowed those two things to win. I took my own power away and squished it up. I didn't write about this last year because it felt too raw, too real and I felt absolutely dismal. I kept my feelings on this limited to a select and trusted few. I could barely cope with the shame and disappointment in my own company, let alone plaster on a facade or wallow in how rubbish I felt in front of people.

The day before the close of the exhibition, I manifested the mother of all migraines. Clearly, I had pushed myself too hard. The culmination of being in my head for too long—anticipating, stressing, worrying and a fear of failure—took over. It took three solid days for that migraine to pass and even longer for the numbness of failure to diminish. I was incredibly hard on myself and the only person who made me feel that way was ME. No one else. Our own expectations are the hardest to exceed and when we fall short, we fall hard. I will still stubbornly describe myself as not being a perfectionist, but clearly the way I was living in my head and beating myself up was perfectionist behaviour. The whole, if it's not done just 'so', I have done badly, it sucks, and I suck.

I had fallen out of love with myself. I wasn't working from the heart; I was working from a place of fear and I allowed it to consume me, and my body responded with a migraine.

I stopped painting for several months and dedicated myself to crafting jewellery and writing. Two passions that haven't, to this day, triggered perfectionism or failure-inducing feelings. I really had lost my zest for painting. I did reclaim it this year and you will see that if you look back at my art posts from March/April. Thanks to an amazing teacher, all-round cool dude and self-taught artist, Jesse Reno. That's a story in the next chapter.

When Gutsy Girl began, I focused on creating art and handmade jewellery, my first jewellery collection was Superpowers: the melding of eco sterling silver forged with earth's crystals. While the jewellery bench is no longer in action, the concept of superpowers remains. My first tagline was all about empowering modern-day heroines. Over the past five years I have been working hard, sinking ever deeper into simply being, studying myself through spiritual and priestess practices, evolving and healing through creative arts and, without ever really knowing what was around the corner, whether I would succeed in my endeavours or not, I was always, always putting faith and trust (sometimes a little, these days a lot) in the precious superpower I was born with: my intuition. If it weren't for this and my never-ending desire and curiosity to see where the path will lead, I would not be here creating and transforming and evolving into the next stage.

I have come full circle, I have worked hard, I have cried buckets and even though I still do not really know for sure where I am headed or what the meaning of life is, I continue to chase my Holy Grail with fervour and passion. Everything I create, absolutely everything, is linked and builds from one thing to the next. I'm a dot connector. I see patterns in everything. I see pain where others see smiles. I see lies when others see truth. I see bullshit when others see brownies. I see shapes in clouds despite the eye rolls. I have a gift and I am using it every single day. I am learning every day.

REFLECTION
QUESTIONS

- Honour your teachers: who taught you?
- Who do you learn from today?
- What have others taught you to love and embrace about yourself?
- What do you long to make and create?
- What creative activities have you enjoyed in the past?
- If you could create anything, what would it be?

9
Heal

'If you have a deep scar, that is a door; if you have an old, old story, that is a door. If you love the sky and the water so much that you almost cannot bear it, that is a door. If you yearn for a deeper life, a full life, a sane life, that is a door.'
—Dr Clarissa Pinkola Estés

My healing journey

My healing journey coincided with what most people tend to call a spiritual awakening. In this chapter, I'll share entries and stories from those years, the modalities I tried and the modalities that continue to support me today.

Keep running up that hill

You've enrolled in a few personal development courses, maybe even hired a coach. You've thought long and hard about it and have decided to dedicate more time to figuring out why you're here and what your gifts and talents are. You are going along your merry way, but you stop suddenly. This personal growth work can be tough. If you felt chewed up and spat out by life when you had no idea who you were or what you were doing before, oh boy, are you in for one hell of a rollercoaster ride!

I'm not trying to scare you off. Far from it. You are here because you want the raw, non-cuddly version of gutsy living that's going to inspire you into action. This may not be the one you wanted. But it might be just what you need.

I've spent the last three and a half years blogging, guest blogging and writing for online publications, and I've read an absolute cacophony of advice blogs. There is so much rich and beautiful wisdom out there, no doubt about it. There are a lot of highlight reels and posts and coming out of the dark into the light. They all have value and an audience who needs it.

One thing that has concerned me in my own blogging and writing experience is worrying about how my message is taken and what people might think. Truth is, it took me a couple of years to actually share myself being raw and real and when I did, I felt so much better and people would contact me to let me know that they appreciated it.

There's always so much talk about being authentic and showing up just as you are. But is everyone who writes about being authentic being their truest and most honest self? I'm not sure. What I know for sure is how I choose to show up in the world. When I'm put on the spot or when I have time to consider my answer, my natural instinct is honesty. I say and write how I feel and think. Sometimes I soften the blow a bit, and other times I'm raw, real and very direct. It's important to be who we are. We all have multi-faceted personalities, and we aren't always in the same mood for the same things.

My intention with anything I do or share is to provoke an action, a new way of thinking, a new belief or practice and to help heal with the messages I serve.

Several times this week I had an all-too-common feeling wash over me. I felt drained, dejected and all 'woe is me'. *Why the fuck am I doing this?* I'm feeling unapologetic about it because I've been hustling and it has driven me to the point where it feels unbearable, and there is no other word I can muster up to explain what I'm feeling in my body right now.

Personal growth is painful. Really painful. I'm often on the brink of tears, madness and losing my usual composed vibe. I can, for the most part, be unshakeable, but then, I slip away from my purpose, mission and core desired feelings. For all the leaps and bounds that occur when making progress, the pain, self-doubt and self-analysis go into overdrive. I need to quieten my mind and gently detach. Get out of my head and back into my body and ask myself, 'what really matters?'

Earlier this week, I questioned myself for the millionth time about whether the hustle and pursuing the work I'm passionate about is worth it. Within two hours of that thought forming I had an impromptu half-hour conversation with someone, and they walked away feeling better and more supported than before we spoke.

Thanks universe. I needed the reminder that YES, all the hustle, self-doubt, falling down and getting back up again (over and over and over) is necessary. It's necessary because the gifts I bring into the world are needed, even if it takes a long time to be seen and heard. Perhaps this resonates with you, too.

For most of my life I made myself the quietest and the smallest, to not be seen or heard. That's the outcome emotional trauma had on me. It made me want to not be seen. It made me want to not be heard. It was easier to be shy and quiet than to stand up alone and be a voice. What could I possibly say that could be of value or benefit to anyone?

While not wanting to be seen or heard was a distinct outcome, it wasn't a conclusion. The decision was not final, and I certainly didn't make the deal.

A few years ago, I awakened something, or perhaps it was the other way around—something awakened me. I'm still not entirely sure. I was searching for something and I pursued it with fervour. I wanted answers and I was prepared to go the distance to get them. I enrolled in so many online classes—a melting pot of creativity, healing and life purpose discovery. I found out who I was when I painted in my art journal and on canvas. Art and creativity were the way I expressed my voice which was still scared to be heard. Intuition is a big part of this transformative work.

I eventually stepped tentatively into the shoes of my true identity and even though I've fought about whether it was the real me or not, I knew that it was. No mistake was made here. My intuition has been a huge beacon and while I denied it for a long time, I know to my core that I am who I am.

Lately my mind has been plagued with questions like, 'am I doing enough?', 'am I doing the right things?', 'is anyone actually getting anything out of what I create?'. I feel truly vulnerable sharing my inner workings. It has occurred to me that I haven't done much of that in this space for quite some time. I've been riffing and telling stories at my in-person events, diverted all my thoughts and feelings there and not given myself the time to write, reflect and share. I love in-person events and how I can just roll with the conversation and what is needed.

I'll say it again. Personal growth is painful. But you need to feel it. You need to be in this place. I promise you, it will make sense.

Sometimes it gets dark within (my heart, my soul). I second-guess myself and my life purpose many more times now that I'm an awakened soul with goals and dreams than when I was too afraid to try. There is no 'too afraid' for me now. The purpose of all this inspiration, all this stress, all this hustling and all this constant work to the point of exhaustion (hello, the past week and a bit) is because my intention when working with others is for them to walk away feeling and knowing that the choices they make to be happy are their choices, that their happiness hinges not on what others think of them but what they think of themselves.

In the midst of deep healing and painful personal growth, I can still say that all of this is worth it. You have to crack open, even if you feel like you are breaking open in order to up-level your life. You have to see that you are worth the time for this unfolding and recalibration of yourself to take place and make way for a bigger and bolder future that only you have the power to create.

Behind gutsy gatherings

When I decided to create a workshop experience, compassion was top of the list because it is my empathic and highly sensitive nature that connects me to every being I meet. I talked about how being a sensitive and 'feeling' person can be 'too much' for many, and how I've learned to embrace it as my superpower. Compassion is what I feel when people share their stories with vulnerability. Compassion is how I feel when someone stumbles but manages to overcome their challenges. Is compassion your superpower too?

Gutsy Gatherings are connective experiences specifically created to cultivate relationships with kindred spirits. I saw this and more on Friday. I led the group to close their eyes, call in their intention and listen to my reading of *The Invitation* by Oriah Mountain Dreamer.

We talked about feelings, how we feel and want to feel, accepting all parts of ourselves. We acknowledged that everyone is a teacher and that words of inspiration and motivation are just as much for the teacher as they are for the reader or listener. We spoke of the need to be vulnerable about feelings of failure and about seeking and trying out different creative hobbies, making ugly art and incomplete canvases, but to always keep going anyway.

When I looked around the room as everyone closed their eyes to listen to music or a reading, I was in awe of everyone. I felt for everyone. How they showed up, how some came along even though they didn't know what they would get from the experience, how some had an inkling and wanted to know more, or deeply felt and have read what I share and felt compelled to attend. I was stunned and humbled when they shared something of themselves, bravely and courageously in a room filled with new friends.

My favourite part of the evening was when I explained the power of 'I AM' statements and led everyone to get creative with coloured pens and markers and write their own powerful I AM statements in the form of Gutsy affirmation cards. This followed with exchanging their mantra cards with other people in the room. Ah, connection! When we exchange the cards, which hold the messages we want to tell ourselves, we discover how similar we all are. We realise that we also struggle with the same things. I loved the discussion when a few people spoke about the story behind why they wrote their chosen I AM affirmations.

Compassion is feeling for other people in a way that raises the vibration of all humanity. Connecting and having the ability to feel someone's tears or experiences and to send love. You don't have to know someone well or even see someone in person to feel compassion. Compassion has no limits, and I hope for a world where we all act more compassionately towards one another. Compassion and love are true powers. Not greed, war, hate or wealth.

I closed with a beautiful track by Tahlee Rouillon, 'You Already Fly on Wings of Light'.

I am thankful for my husband, Ryan. I call him The Man With The Questions. It was his 'why don't you?' that got this workshop and other gatherings off the ground. I am thankful for my firecracker daughter who emulates what I do and writes her own Gutsy affirmations, so I know I am doing a good job—even though we clash and I often think I am a shit mother. I am thankful for everything that I felt and heard on Friday night. I am thankful for everything that I felt all weekend. I was like a sloth all weekend actually because as the adrenaline wore off, I wanted to simply *be*. I trusted the universe, I trusted myself in ways I never have before and now I don't feel worried about not being enough, or not being capable of holding space for people, or not getting my message across, because I did it. I overcame my silly little fear about public speaking. I was myself, I showed up exactly as I am, I held space so my attendees could share themselves, I was clear in my message and I had faith. Not all of the emotion has released just yet. This post is written with tears welling up in my eyes from sheer joy. I came to this realisation at the weekend and finally felt my power in the core of my being, something that was lost for a long time:

> I am not afraid;
> I was born to do this.
> —Joan of Arc

Find yourself

Earlier in my adult life, I endured relationships which suffocated me. I couldn't grow, be myself or be outspoken like I am now. Looking back, I allowed myself to be stifled and I did so because I didn't think I was worthy of anything better. When you are young, there is a tendency to not look too far ahead. You don't see the possibilities or greener pastures that could lie ahead of you if only you gave to yourself, instead of somebody else. You stay in jobs that fucking suck, where you work your arse off for low pay, no recognition or gratitude. You stay in relationships where you are disrespected, cheated on, manipulated and gaslit into thinking that it is you not them who is at fault and that you deserve your misery and depression. Allowing someone else to control and be the voice of your inner narrator. It's a vicious weapon and over time, internalises and tarnishes how you show up in the world.

If I could offer any piece of wisdom to any reader younger than myself, it would be this:

- You don't have to accept a lower standard just because you don't feel worthy of more yet.
- You don't have to stay in that job that pays you little but expects so much of you.
- You don't have to stay friends with someone who, after catching up with them, you feel drained and exhausted because they sucked the good energy from you.
- You can make a better choice, one that prioritises your wellbeing and worth.

Finding yourself and growing yourself without limit, edit or censorship while in a relationship is a rare and beautiful thing. I'm fortunate to have the partnership and marriage I have and to be with someone who has only ever cheered me on and celebrated my growth.

There were times I was afraid during these periods of personal and spiritual growth and healing post-motherhood. Would we grow apart? How much could our union stand if I kept evolving? Could I outgrow us?

REFLECTION QUESTIONS

- What learning and lessons have you integrated into your being?
- What of these things you've learned are holding you back?
- What have you learned that doesn't resonate with you any longer?
- What are the gaps in your learning and healing journeys?
- What would healing from what ails you enable you to feel?
- What healing remains to be addressed?
- What action can you take towards healing (as it means to you)?

10
Fierce Devotion

'Just living is not enough. One must have sunshine,
freedom, and a little flower.'
—Hans Christian Andersen

Boundaries. The first realisation of wavering boundaries is noticing that something either drains you or sustains you. Which is it?

Tired, overwhelmed, burned out, sensory overload. I suspended nourishment and temporarily forgot to exert some of that sensitive superpower goodness—compassion and love—on myself. Have you been here?

I've learned that it takes time to nourish ourselves fully. My nourishment is still unfolding. I am a one hundred-hour candle lighting up the dim and the din. I am a slow burn, a meltingly blurred waxiness in pools of golden light. I think we often forget that last part in the culture of hustle and rush. Not the waxiness part, but the slow-burning quality of you and me. Each has our own candle of burning time and birthing brilliance. While in the phase of creation, we can think what is taking shape is really shit because we haven't got the miles to witness its full evolution, the evolution of each of us. Intersecting and integrating paths, Gutsy Leaders do not allow themselves to be weighed down with the burden of thoughts about our life being of late harvest qualities. We take the time to appreciate what we have reaped, infusing our love and fiercest devotion to something we may not be able to describe in words because, right now, it is a full sensory feeling. Ecstatic.

It's your favourite songs blasted.

It's the song that you always dance to.

This is the breadth of a life I wish for you.

I wish for you the countless hours of joyous play and creation.

The beauty and texture of slow, simmering burn.

Brilliance that melts like gold.

A winding path that is always exciting, potent and lush.

Moment of pause, reset and rebirth.

Your highest truth is always expanding.

The song in your heart, eternal.

Boundless energy and bountiful boundaries.

Your formidable quest is taking shape.

Stages of unravelment

Unravelling entertainment. Many a moment for musing at the times life innately throws you black comedy based on your life. As I named it in the 'Belonging' chapter, chainsaws were the sensation of teen and adulthood. Each journey of unravelment contains various stages, and some on high rotation.

It seems I like to start my next unravelment quest while feeling burned out.

Leaning into leadership

I've learned through mistakes, life lessons, relationships, friendships, core wounds and trauma, busting through every fear, real and imagined, while starting and building a business that matters. I have learned through trials and tribulations that commitment is mandatory. Commitment has been staring me in the face and has been right on my bedside for several months following a breakthrough message and healing with my kinesiologist. I read that 2014 postcard message every day for a while, waiting for it to sink in. I had to feel my way through to becoming my own champion and it wasn't going to happen overnight or with repetition. Saying it doesn't make it happen. There's more to the equation. I came to realise that I have been actively working on commitment and acceptance, too, mainly in relation to self.

As if guided by my highest self, I have these messages for you:

As I commit to myself every single day,

I put it out there that I am saying 'yes'.

I'm saying yes to healing myself.

I'm saying yes to my dreams.

I'm saying yes to self-belief and self-trust.

Sometimes I lose faith, but that is just temporary.

It's just a crack in the journey and as long as I continue, I will see myself and my acceptance of self for what it is: aligned with a higher purpose.

I am committed to my path ahead. I may show fear or weakness, but ultimately I know that I am strong.

I am committed to myself. I trust that I have done enough and know enough. I am on my way. I am right where I need to be. I am the embodiment of what is needed for commitment to manifest into abundance and prosperity.

REFLECTION
QUESTIONS

- Boundary review: what boundaries do you need to rein in? What boundaries do you need to make?
- Who/what is draining you?
- Where do you feel drained?

- What sustains you?
- What do you wish for yourself?
- What is unravelling for you right now?
- How do you experience unravelment? What senses are heightened or activated?
- How can you truly let go during this process?
- How can you become your own champion?
- What commitment do you make to yourself moving forward?

11
Writing to Full Expression

'When you stand and share your story in an empowering way, your story will heal you and your story will heal somebody else.'
—Iyanla Vanzant

Beginning

Writing is my number one passion. Above speaking, it's the way that I choose to communicate—like a lot of chapters in this book. As I wrote, I actually spoke. I dictated this chapter, for example, because it's comfortable for me to use my voice when I'm telling my story and then to use that as a basis for the writing I'm going to continue to do. I remember the initial feeling of deciding that I wanted to start a blog. I had no plan or ideas about what kind of content I would write. On some level, I allowed myself to trust what was going to come out. I was both processing and progressing. And I was just at the very beginning of this nine-year journey of self-discovery, of finding myself and also finding joy, creativity and play in life.

I've made no secret during the time of writing this book that my biggest, tightly held dream was to become an author. Now, this dream is coming to fruition. And it's been on my radar for at least thirty years—that I can remember.

I enjoyed writing stories. As a child, I enjoyed reading stories. So, it makes total sense to me that the thing that I have enjoyed the most as a hobby and activity would be writing.

Writing is a wonderful outlet to process our feelings and unravel from the conditioning: the lies and stories that we've been told about who we are. I see writing as being a magical healing tool, spells, if you will. What spells are we going to cast with our words today?

There is so much richness in being able to tell our stories, so let's go a bit deeper into what that involves and means through my lens and what it could look like for you.

Becoming fully expressed

The first guideline to becoming fully expressed is to give yourself permission to be angry.

We are so used to being conditioned by society and by our families that anger is a negative emotion. For those of us who are racialised and melanated, we see it reflected in this particular way: the trope of the angry Black woman. Or, in my experience as a biracial Asian woman, being told that my anger is too much or that I'm overly sensitive. This has been the most common response to my anger that I can recall. There are many entry points to becoming fully expressed and anger was definitely my first entry point. This began when I was very young and I experienced racism and witnessed my mum experience racism for the first time.

I grew up in a household of three and emotion was never suppressed. So, some emotions weren't handled or received very well. But I grew up in a household where at least two of us were highly sensitive people, and therefore, very expressive when given the opportunity to be so.

I first heard the term 'fully expressed' during the art class that I mentioned in the 'Becoming Gutsy' chapter. It wasn't until I heard this phrase that I realised how much becoming fully expressed was #goals for me. It's how I wanted to show up. It's how I wanted my art to be. It's what I wanted my writing to grow into. And I feel, for all intents and purposes, that my writing has matured and grown, and I've given myself that full permission to express myself.

It's a permission that is not easy to grant yourself. Certainly not with all of the messages that we receive about anger, particularly if we identify as women, particularly if we are Women of Colour. I believe anger is a healthy emotion. I've written many times about how I don't judge the perception of my emotion on the spectrum of whether it's positive or negative. All I know is that when I am experiencing an emotion, I am moving through it, and repressing, suppressing or silencing myself does not serve anyone. It doesn't serve me. It doesn't serve my nervous system. And it doesn't serve the people who trust me, who I serve as a coach and mentor.

While anger can be a gateway into expressing other emotions, it's also a healthy one. It's good for us to express our anger, particularly when we are marginalised. And we are so sick of the status quo and what happens in the world. As writers and creatives, it's important for us to access the full spectrum of emotions so that we can give nuance to the characters or people that we write about—so that we can tell our stories without censoring or editing ourselves—we have the opportunity to write, whether that is in digital media or in print, or within the pages of our first published book.

We need to know that it's safe for us to be angry, that when we have the ability to communicate with people in different ways and we receive an opportunity like publishing, we have the urge to go all in and not leave anything out. As I've mentioned in a previous chapter, I don't want my greatest regret in life to be leaving anything left unsaid.

Just write

Just write.

Our words matter, and if you haven't heard that before, I'll remind you again with oomph: your words matter.

Some music just drives me to type faster and match my mind-computer speed. Writing is not just writing. I often audio transcribe my stream of thought and edit them later. Writing is a full-body experience and I often wish that neurotypical people who believe themselves to be grounded, peaceful and embodied to try it my way sometime.

Through writing, I feel everything. I feel the words streaming out from my brain and into the ether, to my fingertips trying to keep up with my thoughts and put them into words on the screen. I feel the music I listen to as I write, and I can often recall music based on what I've been doing at the time. I feel a huge sense of relief, release and peace when I get my words out and they are no longer in the brain tangle of my thoughts, feelings and emotions. As a visual thinker and writer, I see my words as pictures, colours, movements, textures, scents, tastes and something that feels like a complete elevation of spirit.

If you are a music lover, and I hope you become one if you aren't now, I compel you to listen to music across genres and notice the difference in your body when you listen to a ballad versus a political tune. Write what you notice, feel at the time, feel afterwards, anything that that music brought to the surface for you: questions and thoughts, maybe about the lyrics because you were really listening this time. Repeat. Allow this to be your writing activity. Notice when you write, your energetic capacity, time of day, when you are most in flow and evolve your being into that.

I compiled a soundtrack of songs that evoked or provoked the content, reminded me of times long past and brought forth emotions and memories of the time. The tunes serve to expand your genres, different layers and levels of emotions and the combination of voice and instruments.

The voice that gets to express itself fully and how you can too

I've been thinking a lot about music, and beyond the genres, voices and identities of each music artist I have long realised male voices are prominent on my playlists. I'm particularly fond of baritone voices with texture and depth, not just power. My early years in the late 70s and early 80s were spent listening to everything from Boney M to Michael Jackson and Billy Idol before my late-80s interest in Bryan Adams, which has long faded, and led to my foray into hard rock, grunge and alternative music in the 90s. From there, I came of age while listening to my (now) long-time favourites: Nine Inch Nails, Depeche Mode, The Cure, Garbage, Skunk Anansie and Miranda Sex Garden. Seriously, listen to their songs on 'The Soundtrack' (listed in the back of this book) for some incredible voices and lyrics, followed by nu-metal and heavier stuff and old favourites on continual high rotation. It's the emotions and full expression of themselves through their words and their voices that are baked into my being and part of why I feel and think so broadly and deeply without even trying.

The male voice gets to express itself fully with little judgement. That's one of my perspectives now upon decades of observation and listening to male voices and noticing the critique of voices that aren't. We see how expression is played out by the patriarchy, from whose voices get heard, paid and celebrated, to whose voices are speaking up, against oppression and in solidarity but don't get the airplay or recognition.

When I listen to my heavier, angrier tunes, the expression is not just vocal, but an entire bodily function from how the singer moves, emotes and expresses while performing and how something as 'simple' as words are and can be a weapon. I listen to some very fully expressed music and I dance solo a lot, so I know not how the words sound but how the music feels.

If I can help you to connect with your inner writer through another powerful form of expression and communication—music—I'll move forward happier. When I listen to music that provokes me, I can go deeper with greater focus on my writing, allowing it to flow and expand, like the rise and fall of our chests as we breathe, and when I am trying to find the words, the beats and voices give me something to focus and re-focus on. I breathe, I find my centre again, maybe I hook onto a phrase or word in the lyrics and allow it to call some writing to be released.

Music can free us up. Dancing can loosen up our bodies, to sensate and re-connect and re-tune into ourselves, and to get the blood pumping and limbs moving. I also highly recommend a good chair dance, upper body movement, neck stretches, facial movements and expressions; it's all part of it.

Listening to music can help us to release, express, expand and free our thoughts. Sometimes it can take one word or one song that can remind us of a time, memory, story or experience, and the world to write is unlocked for us once more. The best thing is that this can happen any time or multiple times throughout the day. Even five minutes of writing can produce a release, an unlocking of trapped ideas or challenging thought patterns. We have a world of words within us and many other worlds—if we look at music as worlds as well—that are before us to explore and expand into.

Expression also requires silence to aid growth

I noticed myself making plans and taking actions to recoil and remove myself from the online coaching 'industry' for a little while. It happened bit by bit from 2020 when I birthed the Be An Inclusive Coach Program, now known as the Inclusive Coach Recognition Program. A dozen and a half people signed up and a few more people joined Unpack Your Privilege. I dreamt up a big goal and dream I did. I dreamt of a thousand o people who consumed my writing and resources online over the past ten years to partner with me to back my work.

As December 2020 hit, it became real. The hive of activity and fast responses to my call to action in the days after George Floyd, and more Black deaths at police hands, were a mere trend and nowhere near close to becoming a broadening self-aware society and anti-racist humankind. Instead, the numbers were plummeting and yet, I persevered.

Frightened into fear, I looked for employment in the first quarter of 2021. No interviews, one email rejection and a list of no responses. I kept on keeping on.

I set myself a boundary goal to rein mine right in and focus most on what brought me joy, rest, practice and creativity. I faltered on the goal to pare my social media writing way back. That lesson took twelve months to come around again before I integrated it. I inched further and further away from writing about coaching, most things really, as I prepped myself the time and space to devote myself to completing this manuscript.

The world was not my oyster but my rollercoaster again as I toyed once more with finding employment at the end of March 2022 as declining interest in inclusive coaching and unpacking privilege reared its familiar head again and I realised I was burned out, over it, and also neurodivergent. At the same time, I was searching for a new home as our lease was coming to an end, both my husband and I were starting new roles and I was returning to employment after a four-year self-employment stint. Twelve years on from my last job interview, I secured a video interview for a not-for-profit and I got the job. This felt like the tide was finally turning, but stress was high as we had a few weeks to find a new place to live, and the rental market was expensive, limited and competitive. In a three-week daze we packed up our place with no initial idea where we were headed, a rejection, more packing, another inspection, an approval and a move-in date and all services coordinated for the transition.

There was also the matter of finishing this book with its deadline just weeks away. At every waking moment, the thought of writing lay in the foreground of my mind, while executing the task happened during infrequent bursts and blares of typing activity when the mood chose itself. The book, itself, has had a life of its own and many times I wondered after long stints not writing, but pondering and ruminating over details, descriptors and memories, whether it required revival from its grave. Every time I returned to it I felt a new voice of mine was coming through. I sensed a disjointedness with chronology and the non-linear blending together of my potion of words. My brain drove my fingers to type words across the screen, which at times did not make immediate sense and rarely stuck in my memory after they were typed. Upon reading, receiving the humbling surprise of 'when did I write this?' arose a couple of times.

The closer the deadline approached, the more clarity I had. I'm truly amazed. It's been like brewing the perfect pot of tea or allowing a marinade to infuse for depth and intensity of flavour. Good things, the best things, come with and in time. Much of this book I wouldn't have been ready or prepared to write until the final weeks in the lead up to submitting my manuscript.

Writing is so much more than the act of writing itself. This book has involved a large amount of thinking, reflecting and pondering on my life for more than a few years, asking myself over and over, 'how do I say what I want to say?'. I had to train myself to not diminish the amount of time I spent percolating and mulling over what and how to write something and whether I even wanted to put some of these thoughts into print. Writing is liberating. Writing is an act of liberation when we use it with confidence, conviction and courage. Our voices become a part of a rising chorus of self-expression. We aren't alone. There is a state of undoing in removing the silencer from our stories. An unravelling of confusion, an untangling to clarity, unwavering knowing and a responsibility that our stories can be another's undoing and reclamation. My writing voice has tested me in ways I am only comprehending in layers.

REFLECTION
QUESTIONS

- What if my dissenting voice is met with crickets? Do I stop there or find another way?
- Which stories do I unlock from my vault?
- What message or lesson is contained within?
- Which stories are worth retelling?
- Which stories are difficult or uncomfortable but allow me to express myself, process and move forward?
- What healing could be beneath this pain or trauma, if I have the resources to take advantage of it?

I learned that I have to trust the fullness of my expression without quite knowing why or when I feel like I don't have the confidence to persevere. I can't let those factors stop me.

Examining my life and the stories I've shared, I've been able to process, re-process and look back to be kinder to myself and more forgiving. I am toughest on myself even though it might appear I'm fairly tough on others, because I'm idealistic, I am clear on my values, my stance and am innately justice-sensitive with deep empathy. I don't hold others to a standard I am not reaching for or meeting myself. That's to say I want us all to win and be our fullest selves, not full of ourselves. I don't want any spotlight or attention for being fully expressed. For me, it's a whole feeling that courses through my life and way of being. That's what I'm reaching for—a feeling that I cannot describe in words because it has to be felt. I know when I'm in my fullest expression because I feel grounded, calm and liberated, even if the subject is emotive or looks like rage. I have had a lifetime of practising trying to get life right until I decided to just do it my way. Creativity and experimenting with art have helped facilitate and expand my expression. I'm glad this was the foundation on which I crafted my business instead of just being all about a freedom-based lifestyle and hustle culture. I started slowly with art and immersed myself right into it. There is just something about spending hours painting and expressing on paper or canvas that's unparalleled to anything else. It brings focus, colour, vibrancy, texture and mindfulness together, and it's something that anyone can try. You don't need lots of supplies or artist-quality materials. The fun of it is making a mess and remembering child-like play and fun and ceasing to worry about what the outcome is going to be or if you make mud with the colours you've chosen. It's all fun, experimental and freeing.

Heart and rage

Moving from one rental house to another in middle age, after three pandemic years at home and social distancing, old muscles squealed to say 'hi', and I realised not only how tired I had been, but how amazing it was that I filled up all the white space I'd simultaneously cleared with renewed boundaries, unwanted stress and anxiety over moving and adapting to remote work. It hasn't felt like a huge adjustment, more a learning curve as I understand the ropes of the not-for-profit sector instead of the self-employment route. Skills I developed from being self-employed such as learning, researching, developing, creating, facilitating and innovating are useful, adaptive and transferable. What I have noticed is my capacity and my energy. Specifically, how much I have of them both at different times and how I can best leverage them, not to be consistent, but to be aligned with what feels good, joyful, achievable and sustainable—against the epitome of that ableist notion of consistency. I began writing about consistency being ableist before I knew just how ableist I was being towards myself. Closely linked to this are the traits and effects of manipulative marketing, hustle culture and productivity which I cover in my video trainings, Formidable Business and Inclusive Business Retreat.

First of all, the message of consistently posting on social media = ableist. All of us trying to carve a space in the online business world are sold the lie of consistency as part of a manipulative capitalist marketing formula that if we show up CONSISTENTLY on social media that we, too, can have the success of the people who sell that message. It's a lie that's spread so far and wide and by so many that we can easily be convinced that it is true. It's not. The trouble with these messages of consistency is that they are spouted by people who are mostly able-bodied, neurotypical, healthy and well, not to mention non-racialised, non-melanated and accessorised with all that it means to be privileged.

Consistency doesn't suit neurodivergent, disabled or chronically ill people. It doesn't because we just can't. We can't 'keep up' because our conditions and brains don't enable or cater to that default able-bodied neurotypical habit or behavioural setting. Our mind computers are different. Where does that leave us when it comes to visibility and being 'successful'? I have continued to explore these answers as I unpack my neurodivergent life, long after I realised that's what it was the whole time. Consistency is also a message that causes harm. My concern and two questions are:

1.   Shouldn't harm prevention and awareness be brought to the forefront of these marketers' minds?
2.   Why aren't they investing in education to ensure their practices, methods and messages are inclusionary and not exclusionary?

If they are, it's not being integrated or practised. If enrolment is the only action they've taken, it doesn't count. They must be actively doing the work. From my perspective, this doesn't seem widely adopted.

I explain and identify what I call 'junk food capitalism and marketing' in the Formidable Business component of my body of work.

Notice how consistency messages trip you up. Do only what you can and feel capable of doing. Show up in a way that befits you and honours your capacity.

There are many examples of ableist society, manipulative marketers and hustle and productivity culture. You don't need to fall for their myths and lies to get your message across (you don't have to hire them, either!). Focus on following your dreams and passions, bring your vision to life and throw away their rulebooks and formulas.

If everywhere on social media you see products and services sold by neurotypical white influencers and coaches, and they are marketing themselves as the 'norm' or having the best solutions, it doesn't mean this is true. It doesn't mean it's right, accessible, good or inclusive for anyone. It's worth stating here, too, that racialised and melanated people, despite our intersections, can also be ableist and exclusionary.

I've learned from my experiences and taken away very little learning from such white influencers and coaches. Why? Mainly because I write for a community of diverse people including marginalised, chronically ill, disabled humans, with whom I share these identities. No one is better placed or informed than those of us who have the lived experience, empathy and understanding of these layers. I have personally unpacked the lies we have been told that condition us to feel bad or inadequate for being who we are and being unable to perform at a consistent and steady pace. Our pace must be set to our abilities and capacity, not some default, unreasonable and ableist standard that we can never meet.

Rest affirmation

Rest is a hot topic with my clients. It comes up in most one-on-one coaching calls as well as group coaching calls I facilitate. I feel that's quite telling. Our bodies are messengers, and we receive the message, but because of societal conditioning, numbing out, repressing or suppressing our feelings, what we consume on these social media grids regarding hustle and bootstrapping and what we've been led to believe about work 'culture' and capitalism, we don't take the message on board to follow through on rest or sleep until the burnout alarm bell rings.

Take this rest affirmation and sit with or nap on it today:

Radical rest is my birthright. The more rest I give myself permission to take, the better my boundaries, energy, discernment and work in the world can become.

Give yourself ten minutes to expand into it. Take a nap if you are able. I sometimes listen to binaural beats to help my brain even while I am working and creating. It's so soothing. Music can be regenerative.

Side note: I wrote much of this book listening to adding to my book writing playlist, many of the songs ended up being the anthems featured in 'The Soundtrack'.

Rest looks different for each of us. To an outsider who isn't dismantling their conditioning and beliefs, it could look like 'laziness'. We are damned (by others) if we do, we are damned (by ourselves) when we don't! There are days when my body screams at me to stop doing all the things. I don't always listen. Do I pay for it with days and sometimes weeks of migraines, brain fog and other symptoms of stress!? Yes.

It takes practise to pause and rest, listen to our body wisdom and tune out the laziness BS. I'm getting better at it despite my mind's BS about laziness, consistency and progress. The burnouts I've experienced have been big lessons and illuminated that listening to my body over my mind is its best compass/GPS.

We get praised for being hard workers, doing double time, working on weekends (whether we are employees or work for ourselves), but where is the cheering when we rest and take a break? If you say yes to your body and rest, I'm cheering you on from the sidelines (and on some days, from my bed office).

Stalling forward

I feel myself stalling. Putting off big decisions. Putting off my current big decision to finish this book.

A deadline has helped somewhat, but wow, who knew that resistance and procrastination could be this intense. Feeling intensely is always my state of mind. It's exhausting how I managed to keep it going for years, coupled with anger and passion as I wrote my heart out on racism, representation, inclusion, racial and social justice, on what most months felt like the smell of an oily rag. I was running on empty constantly and doing little to recharge myself beyond my essential monthly massages, which I had to keep up even when funds were tight.

Energetically, I was scattered, and my compulsive writing habits were winning while on the inside I was losing. My writing was compulsive and also proactive, as much as going over past events can be. My desire to do better means showing up and offering writing and services to broaden and shape others' minds about anti-oppression and anti-racism.

I was still holding down my day job which was always busy, and a place in which I had grown ever vigilant and discerning of who I engaged with. Every December, it was the same last-minute activities and a mad rush of must-do work before Christmas Eve. I was over it. Who the hell designed this work schedule and workload that came to the same crescendo every December? 'Why can't things be done differently?', was my evergreen internal question.

At the last office Christmas party before my redundancy, I realised I had to get the fuck out of there when a weapons project was lauded and celebrated. People clapped. I was struck by how sickening that was. I saw no cause for celebration. All I knew was that it was a project I was assigned to work on. My values? I knew what they were, and the company where I was spending five days a week was far from them. A few weeks later, I experienced racism from my non-racialised relatives. This stung the roots of my being. By that stage I had been writing online about social justice for six months as I explored what I was learning and what I planned to do about it.

I observed the somewhat tokenistic twelve days of gender equality at my former workplace and watched as another year sailed by stuck in mud thanks to misogyny and other bullshit. After years of being told to 'come out of my shell more', with no advice or help offered, talk of my 'potential', doing as I was instructed, sharing a cubicle office cell (hell) with a toxic, gaslighting sexist and told that I was being sensitive and had misinterpreted the communication, I was tired of trying on somebody else's terms. People who look like me can work their arses off, do what we are told, follow instructions to the letter, be assertive and speak up, show expertise and leadership and still fall short of the ever-moving finish line. Who was eligible to get to the finish line was clear. Without sounding like a flake, I felt destined for expansive potential and answers, not whatever this was.

A few months later I was called to a meeting with someone who I previously worked with. My internal question was how were they ever going to top me finding out that I had been reassigned to another division via PowerPoint presentation? I knew where this particular conversation was heading, and I was prepared for it. Here comes the reality version of my incredible shrinking desk story. As I stood at the doorway, I immediately spotted the manila folder on the desk and I knew it contained my latest fate: redundancy number two. I knew in my bones that it was coming some six weeks earlier after it was announced that the company would 'restructure'. In my eight years, there was one approximately every eighteen months and several disruptive desk moves during my tenure.

The ever-smug HR person who breached my confidentiality and disclosed my health conditions to my abuser was now in the room to gloat. Were conversations, professionalism and empathy really that difficult to execute? These were the examples of people around me and I'm glad their poor form never rubbed off on me. I have done my best throughout my life to ensure that I don't emulate what I was shown or how I was treated in the many workplaces in which I was employed. It's essential that we allow that growth, no matter how long and how much practise it takes. I just wondered why they took so long to find a way to get me gone after the 'trouble' I caused by my complaint against a manager whose behaviour was gaslighting and therefore abusive? I felt a part of me that had shut down to cope with the workplace-originated PTSD could start to breathe again. I was going to be out of there soon enough. I told my former colleague who handed me my redundancy letter that I saw this coming. He was shocked. I guess humans are the species that embody the ostrich myth of heads in the sand. We can sit in the same room and still have no idea about what's going on around us unless it affects or benefits us.

I've come to the realisation that stalling hinders me, and while I feel my own resistance, I somehow always find a way to move through it, however painful, exasperating and deepening an experience it is.

I was designed to go deep into whatever I turned my hand and mind to. Recognising this means I can stay true to myself, my values and my vision.

Diversion incursion

After working so long while stretching myself too thin, I created spaces and places to explore my interests and soul through events, community and teaching. I'm currently on another diversion incursion where I'm re-examining lessons in learning and trying to put them into practice. I'm paring back on what I deliver and offer as services. I'm giving myself permission to take each day as it comes and respond to my special interests and limit the number of my new projects. Writing this book is my long-term project during 2022. I know it will require a lot of me and will test me beyond my comfort zone. I ricochet between *fuck it, I'm doing it*, to *will this provide joy, practice, rest, nourishment, creativity?* This is what I must do to emerge and grow into who I'm here to be. Is it time for cookie me, yet?

The price of speaking out in friendship

It's not until we begin raising our voices, speaking up as leaders and claiming space, that we realise just how much we are capable of holding space for. The space to grow and heal is often in tandem with coaching, teaching and doing our work in the world. While writing this book, I finally came to this item on my long 'to do eventually' list, and that was to take some time to reflect upon the past five years of intensive unlearning, relearning, creation, teaching and growth.

There are many prices we pay for choosing to speak out. But first, some of our speaking out comes from silence. Being silenced by others who feature in our story; being silent because the traumatic experiences and pain we've felt left no room for anything else but to keep going and repress the pain; being silent because we are in denial or are questioning all we've been conditioned to believe about ourselves and others; being silent because we value comfort over making real change.

In the process of speaking out, we become familiar with another aspect of pain: when people we love seek to mute our message and gaslight our story, experiences, thoughts, feelings and opinions, and become people who we thought they weren't. For me, this has been a wound that hasn't quite healed yet.

I've learned that people come and go throughout various stages of our lives. Sometimes their departure is painful and surprising, other times we just 'knew' it would boil over one day. It took me a long time to integrate that lesson. On the ones that helped me grow the most, I have been able to look back with full peripheral vision. I know what role I played in these shifts.

Year 12 of high school ended with a bang. Loss, grief, alongside a 'thank fuck that experience is over'. I realised that all my friends and I were moving in different directions and not towards each other. It wasn't spoken about or discussed, it just happened. We stopped phoning one another and one time, I didn't answer the door. I didn't handle the result of my Higher School Certificate very well and when it came to my high school friends, I shut them out. I retreated as I've come to learn I do when I feel ashamed, disappointed, unworthy or like a failure. I was changing, we all were, and I had my sights on other places, seeking belonging and understanding with no idea of what the future held. We'd turned eighteen, and with our bags of childhood trauma, we grew apart. Almost two decades later we found each other again on Myspace or Facebook.

I was in my mid-twenties when, my then-best friend stood me up when my life was at a beautiful turning point. Beneath it all, we had just grown apart. Her interests were changing; I didn't want to let go. We had a deep friendship, we saw each other wholly, and not speaking after five years of close friendship stung.

In the late 90s I house-shared with two very good friends. It was my first out-of-home experience and honestly, I could've done better. We all could have. We were in relationships where we each were gaslit, manipulated and mistreated, and this spilled out into the way we treated each other. It was awful. We were so young and finding our way in the world. The lack of respect we experienced in our relationships with men transferred to how we treated each other. Our communication became notes, slammed doors, silent treatment, whispers behind each other's backs and, in under a year, our living arrangement became untenable.

One Saturday morning in January of that year, I'd had enough. I didn't want to live with them anymore. I moved back in with my parents and regrouped. It was the change in scenery I needed as I ended up leaving the relationship that tarnished our friendship. Thankfully, with time, maturity and growth, we reconnected and developed a stronger friendship years later that continues today. Who knew that from a demise of a friendship we could give one another grace, apologies and forgiveness and rebuild something stronger, better and greater? Today, this is my most valued sisterhood friendship. No one knows me better. We support and love each other, motivate one another, have the best chats and foodie weekend trips, and somehow know the exact thing to say to raise each other's spirits when life challenges us. We grew apart and now we get to grow old together. You know who you are, and I love you.

Over a decade ago, a work colleague became a dear friend who I supported through a scary experience she had with another work colleague. I knew everything about her family and extended family, her life and her dreams. I thought we were on the same page. But I realised she didn't know me anywhere near as well. I didn't talk about some things. I was also far too interested in the lives of others and caring for them to bother anyone with my issues.

As has been one of the recurring themes of my life, I don't often share too much about myself mainly because I'm working through it solo. I didn't know how to call people in. I was always reluctant to ask for help. A few years after we relocated from Sydney to Brisbane, I had to face my dormant demon of trauma and communicated this to my inner semi-circle (it was that small then). This particular friend delivered a cutting blow once I shared my story. She told me that she was not my counsellor. I knew that she wasn't, had never treated her as such, and at this vulnerable point of my life, it was a heavy blow. She complained about the length of my emails which, when I investigated, were often much shorter than hers. I was trying to find facts in what remained of this friendship. It was painful, but I had to let this one go. This was a time where I learned about reciprocity and how overdelivering in friendship serves only one person, and it's not the giver. I didn't want her to be my counsellor, I wanted her to be a friend who listened, just as I was a listener and supporter to her when she needed it.

I have had a number of intense friendships throughout my life. I always tried to look out for my friends. Loyalty meant a lot to me and wasn't always a two-way street. Friendships can get complicated like any relationship. All of them broke my heart more than any relationship I'd ever been in, so that's saying something. Sisterhood meant a lot to me. I failed and made mistakes that I still cringe about to this day. In some instances, I was filled with regret and in others felt a sense of grief and loss. I believe in owning my shit. I experienced coldness and some instances of no accountability when two strong minds were at the opposite ends of disagreements. I wanted no part in any deception and I have my fair share of secrets I will always keep on behalf of others. I felt a lot of grief for the loss of a few friendships that headed downward so rapidly; I was clueless until reality hit. I look back on some friendships and I know that there were things we both could have done differently if we knew what we wanted, if we expressed ourselves with honesty, if we had our needs met, shown empathy when it was needed and been accountable to one another.

In our youth, immaturity, naivety and being all up in our feelings often means friendships can be hard to maintain. It took me many years to process that friendships aren't forever. Sometimes people are only in the transit lounge of our lives. Sometimes stepping away and coming back with fresh eyes, maturity, honesty, truth and love can rebuild a friendship we thought was once broken.

In our adulthood and parenting years, life and careers cause us to embrace the busy and we attempt to seek the exciting in the midst of the mundane, not always thinking about the cost to us and others. We may forget that others have feelings, too, so we do our best to build our empathy skills.

What I've learned through these and many other friendships and relationships is to listen to my intuition. Don't delay if there's an issue and communicate clearly and openly even if it is hard. Be kinder in how we hold space for others and ourselves, allow space and time to grow, heal and forgive, instil better boundaries around how we wish to be treated, who we let in, what we share and how we interact with each other.

Who are they?

They call me outspoken.
They say I'm intimidating.
They say they don't like me.
They want me to say it nicer or just shut up.
They call me racist slurs at the school entrance.
They told me I was useless.
They told me I deserved it.

Who are 'they'? They are many different people, and not one of their opinions matters even though they sting a bit, and their words are used as intentional weapons to cause pain, erase, silence, provoke and encourage trauma and hurtful reactions and damaging emotions.

I wasn't always outspoken. I didn't always use my voice. I didn't always express my opinion. I didn't always use my voice against injustice and hate. I was silent for a very long time. The words stung and stuck, and I allowed myself to become small and retreat into my shell where it was safe and I felt like I belonged.

It was through the freedom and liberating practice of painting and making art that I found my voice. It was through writing my vulnerabilities and stories on a blog that led me on a journey of identity, healing, worthiness and finding my purpose. I was not prepared for this new rollercoaster on my ride through life, but whoever is?

Becoming fully expressed is a form of becoming that, if omitted, would cause my story to be incomplete. I believe in doing what's necessary to become the fullest expression of oneself and that becoming is different for everyone. Reflect on ways you have become something from the trials and challenges of life. Was it something someone said that floored you, stopped you, froze you into silence in order to reduce the largeness of who you truly are?

Becoming fully expressed as I am now didn't begin with the stories I tell today. They began with art and paint, freedom of expression, tactile touch, experimenting, mark-making with ink, charcoal, watercolour, acrylic, metal, hammer, anvil, oils, wax, clay, brushes, red pens, fingers and palms.

12
Inclusion and Becoming Anti-Racist

'Oppressive language does more than represent violence;
it is violence; does more than represent the limits of knowledge;
it limits knowledge.'
—Toni Morrison

Becoming anti-racist

I wish I could start off this chapter by saying that the choice to become anti-racist was entirely mine and not one that came about because of pain, harm, trauma, abuse and verbal violence. Unfortunately, it wasn't. I had to draw a line and set a boundary that meant I had to honour my values, ethics and the principles I live by and say goodbye to people who weren't aligned with my ethics, values and lived experience as a Person of Colour. Sadly, that meant saying goodbye to some of my relatives.

I mistakenly thought for a lot of my life that I was truly seen as a biracial person, that my difference was obvious enough for people to recognise racism. But what it has meant is that I made painful discoveries over the past decade that showed me who people really are. In the words of Maya Angelou, 'When someone shows you who they are, believe them the first time.'

Making the discovery that blood kin and unrelated connections hold racist attitudes, beliefs and stereotypes set me onward to the path of anti-racism and social justice while also navigating my own healing journey of racial trauma, both past and in progress. I have always been someone who seeks the best in people. I worked in the recruitment industry for a number of years in my early twenties and the people-first approach was something that continued to inform me long after I left that industry. Little did I know that racist beliefs lay dormant in people, in family who had shown me immovable and clearly defined ethics and values from a young age when it came to animals but not, as it turns out, to Humans of Colour. If a lesson could sting, this lesson burned and was physically and emotionally painful. This is a pain that hasn't entirely departed.

In January 2018, I learned a painful lesson. Before I begin telling this story, I must preface it with this note: I didn't know at the time or anytime thereafter before the writing of this book about how impacted I was to learn and be confronted by racism from my white family members, or how long it would take me to recover and heal from the pain caused. At the time of writing this chapter, it has been over three years since I cut off any contact with three white women relatives.

During the prepping and writing stages of creating this book, I was completely overwhelmed by stories that could not only fill this chapter, but an entire book, of the racism I have encountered throughout my life, and how those encounters stacked up beyond my counting over the past three years since I claimed anti-racism coach as one of the roles I was becoming. In 2017, I joined some mixed social justice spaces at a time I was processing trauma—racial and otherwise—and seeking communities that were more diverse in representation than the ones I had frequented online over the previous six years. Unfortunately, one that I was a part of was white-led and imploded massively, namely by harming Black women. I couldn't abide by the harm and pain I witnessed and what ensued thereafter. From there onwards, I sought Black-led social justice groups and hired predominantly Black, Indigenous and Asian-led coaching, professionals and membership spaces. I followed more people whose identities and stories I related to, who were speaking my language and expressing the emotions I felt. It was completely transparent to me that a white-led space was not a safe nor a brave space for anyone of colour when white accountability fell drastically short of repair and apology.

Fractured family

I learned a lesson in early 2018 that rocked me. The line spoken by Jensen Ackles as the character Dean Winchester in the TV show *Supernatural* illustrates, 'Family don't end with blood.'

The sign that urged me to dive deep into anti-racism was due to an online exchange of comments and DMs on social media with family members. We disagreed on a few matters regarding Rose McGowan and whether white supremacy exists, and basically a bunch of white decrepitude, aka white fragility, ensued with name-calling behind my back, which I ultimately found out about. I get that several family members and friends saw the comments that were made and were shocked and not equipped to know what to say. The friends that did? Two Black friends and a white school friend came to my defence. I'm thankful for them because they tried, they laboured on my behalf, and they showed me friendship and allyship.

It is hard to write about it now four years later. It still hurts on some level. I could never have imagined that the final catalyst to go down the anti-racist path was because I experienced firsthand microaggressions, and what I felt at the time was extraordinary apathy, from blood relations, which shocked me to my core. Two of the three relatives involved were my early teachers when it came to making a stand against animal testing and cruelty for animal rights. It was bracing coming to the realisation that their empathy and compassion for animals was significantly deeper than that for melanated and racialised humans, including me. Also, how could they not extend their humanity to understand my perspective and the fact that white supremacy is rampant? I do not know if their views, behaviour or position on this matter changed or not, because it was a hard-fought lesson to cut ties and protect myself from further harm since, in my mind, anti-oppression was the only way forward or away from people, no matter who they once were to me.

I grieved the loss of family, and the feeling of estrangement has been very difficult, painful and uncomfortable. I lived halfway around the world from them and had no one but my parents when I was growing up. I travelled there three times, saving my hard-earned money to visit them. One of the relatives was someone who I was quite close to despite the distance. We wrote long letters to each other all through our teen years and early adulthood. We spent Northern Hemisphere summers together when I travelled halfway around the world to visit them and our family there. We were, I thought, like two peas in a pod until that day on Facebook in January 2018. Each of them were encouragers and supporters of me and my work until I moved into doing anti-racism work. I had another relative call me out on Instagram a couple of years later asking why I was blocking family members when I was being 'so nice' to strangers. My brief response referenced the racist behaviour directed at me from her family unit and, sadly, another cord was cut and she unfollowed me. It was less effort for them to deny and shame me than it was to take stock of their behaviour and be accountable for the pain they caused.

Confronting racism and racist attitudes is difficult, painful and traumatic, more so when it is family who you once loved and trusted. I felt betrayed. It made me wonder how they could have pretended for so long. The spark that ignited the end of our relationship was because I took a stand about white supremacy, which they benefit from and didn't like me acknowledging. Imagine defending a famous white woman you don't even know and harming your racialised relative instead?

It took me close to two years to tell my dad what had happened. It was his relations that brought this racial trauma onto me. My family and I were visiting my parents in Sydney before the pandemic struck and we were dining at the Sydney Rowing Club. How could I tell Dad that I was now estranged from three of our relatives because they expressed racism and stabbed me in the back because I was audacious enough to call it out? I feared that Dad wouldn't side with me, even though that really didn't make any sense because he was always in my corner willing to defend me, and would never have my racial identity reduced to slurs and derogatory names. I won't forget the look of disgust and anger on his face when he saw how much it took for me to tell him. My ma was unimpressed and unhappy about what had happened, too. Unimpressed, but not surprised.

Spicy like sambal

When it comes down to it, four years on, I'm spicy like sambal and, therefore, not for everyone. I wish I'd learned this lesson much earlier because it would've saved a lot of heartache. As a lighter skinned, biracial human, I've had to grow a thick skin my whole life, constantly explaining myself and needing to expand my boundaries more than I ever thought would be necessary, especially with people who I thought were better than they are.

Non-melanated and non-racialised people talk a good game, they love being seen as kind and caring when it comes to animals and matters that are important to them that personally affect them, but through my anti-racism and anti-oppression writing and work, I've questioned their belief in their goodness. I've challenged non-melanated and non-racialised people daily with my words on anti-racism and inclusion and, despite my extensive knowledge and lived experience and sharing of facts, they use a host of behaviours and actions that serve to uphold the white supremacy that enables them to be as they are in society. I have learned that when it comes down to it, non-melanated and non-racialised people will always fiercely defend themselves over and above racialised and melanated people. Their reliance on being a 'good person' and being the 'default' in society means they'll largely put themselves first with little care for anyone who is othered. I will caveat this so I'm being clear; of course, I don't mean all non-melanated and non-racialised people. I mean the non-melanated and non-racialised people who debate with racialised and melanated people, who question history and facts with a side of aggression, bias and harmful engagement.

In this book, I'm sharing life through my lens and experiences. Many of the more serious racist experiences I've had (and by serious, I mean threats and other abusive behaviours and ways of communicating) were done with intention and little regard for me or my humanity, my life, experiences and traumas caused by my mere presence among non-melanated and non-racialised people and were done to harm or traumatise me in some way.

I've grown stronger through dozens of direct experiences of racist and bigoted people in the online world. It didn't have to be this way.

If an experience or opinion delivered by a racialised and melanated person causes you to think, causes you discomfort and questions your privilege and level of entitlement, isn't it time you stopped to listen and learn instead of resorting to abusive behaviour?

I would like to imagine that I'm preaching to the choir here. You made a conscious decision to pick up my book and I hope I'm taking you on a journey that's going to guide you to begin to unpack—or unpack more deeply—your anti-racist awareness.

Weight of the world

Being a racialised person who is always praised for my 'resilience' and 'strength' irritates the shit out of me. Do non-racialised people ever even think about where our resilience and strength comes from? Often, I don't think so and my view on this has barely changed since what I witnessed and observed in 2020. Say hello to the oppressive systems that affect us all (and benefit many) differently depending on our unique identities and experiences.

Allow me to put it into words and explain it a little.

So, you've experienced a trauma/s, or series of hardships and challenges and you survived them, maybe even thrived after those experiences and people label you or say things like 'You are SO strong', 'You'll get through this, you're so resilient'. This is meant as a compliment but I don't view it this way. Perhaps you've even used these descriptors for yourself and they accurately describe a pair of your many, many traits.

For racialised people, we experience all kinds of challenges, hardships and trauma, and those experiences aren't a monolith, they are unique to each of us. On top of all this, we also experience racism and racial trauma, erasure, exclusion, appropriation and profiteering of our cultures, and the subsequent denial, decrepitude/fragility, silencing, erasure and manipulative tactics to get us to shut up etc., all by the sword of non-racialised and non-melanated people.

Being described as strong and resilient, in my opinion and experience, reduces and erases the totality of my lived experiences of racism and racial trauma, every traumatic experience and all that it takes for me to keep myself alive. English dictionaries and thesauruses full of words and these are the pick of the bunch? Puh-lease. No thanks.

Expand your vocabulary. Really listen to, learn and integrate what you read and hear from us and reduce the use of these words (resilient, strong) to describe racialised people. In particular, I notice Black women being described in this way and of the Black women I am connected with, they are beyond such basic description. There's no word count on acknowledging Black women as queens and paying them for their work and via reparations.

Racialised people are so much more than just resilient and strong. Maybe get to know us a bit better (if we let you) and you'll find out yourself and find better words to celebrate and compliment us with.

Is apathy your obstacle to anti-racism education?

Under the smokescreen of caring, wanting to help and coach people and giving the appearance of being kind, inclusive and of service, the biggest obstacle I have faced when it comes to talking with and cultivating anti-racists in the non-racialised and non-melanated is their apathy. The measure of someone's apathy initially gives me a snapshot into how these dialogues are going to go and whether the person is genuinely receptive to learning and evolving. I've had my fair share of lip service when people make a point of contacting me via message or email to let me know what their big plans are to become anti-racist. Ninety-nine percent of the time this is the only action they take after letting me know they can't afford to pay me or that they'll just discuss it with their all-white friends (seriously, this happened!) and years later, I see no change in their outlook, beliefs or messaging they put out into the world. Alarmingly, I've seen it go further away, from their current embracing and loving their white privilege to becoming more extreme, denying race and that racism exists and following it up with some transphobia, conspiracy theories or eugenics.

Are these really the leaders we want to aspire to become, when they avoid every uncomfortable conversation about racism and their part in upholding white supremacy? When their first move is harm and not kindness? Do we really want to pay them for goods and services knowing the foundation of who they are and the fact that their business is built on the sandy shores of Strategic White Womanhood[2] and white supremacy?

We want real change, but I know from my experiences with such women, that their desire for change is limited, not limitless, and they won't take the word of a racialised and melanated person who they deem formidable, intimidating and angry when they still haven't completed Self-Awareness 101. Their 'ascension and enlightenment' comes with shallow parameters of not choosing a coach or teacher who is honest, factual and direct, instead only seeking platforms, coaches and teachers that still allow them to be on pedestals, visible to anyone who pays notice and claiming they are doing the work. Perhaps one of the main barriers to an inclusive industry is them?

What do you need to DO and LEARN to stop upholding the gender binary, racism, oppression and capitalism?

I'll throw you a bone: it's not just words on your bio, a statement on your sales page or website. It's self-awareness, education, daily ACTION and, wait for it: accountability, integrity AND practise.

Are you willing to do all of that?

If not, we aren't in this together.

Unpack your privilege framework

It was on a flight to Melbourne for a weekend priestess retreat where I wrote the outline for what was to become Unpack Your Privilege®. I wrote out the steps I personally took to realise my internal anti-racist beliefs and the pathway to unpacking identity, race and privilege. Within two months I had created the first two classes of the framework, starting with the development of two classes: Self-Awareness, and Activism and Action.

The Self-Awareness class covers unpacking social identity, privilege, patriarchy, prejudice, biases, stereotypes, beliefs, challenging beliefs, empathy and empathy building.

I created Activism and Action with empaths and highly sensitive people in mind because that's how I identified at the time. Today, knowing that I'm autistic, I'd describe Activism and Action as being for neurodiverse humans also. Activism and Action involved unpacking key limitations and motivations, commitment and presence, powerlessness, sensitive superpowers, empathic bias, sustainable self-plans and envisioning the world you'd like to live in and your legacy.

To expand on Self-Awareness, I created the Expansion class in early 2019. Expansion built on Self-Awareness and Activism and Action, and includes my approach and models for this work, expanding awareness, spheres of influence, effective solidarity and communication, 'white fragility' and case studies.

In late 2019, I added Spirituality and Social Justice to the framework, which was brought about from my observations and experiences of bringing social justice awareness into spirituality and coaching spaces online and analysing the biases, beliefs and behaviours of non-racialised people.

In 2020, I created the Formidable Business class, analysing the industries I work across, from coaching to spirituality and wellness, to offer practical advice, tips and strategies for identifying white supremacy and manipulative marketing in business practices.

In my Formidable Business workshop, I share the information that racialised and melanated women and people are the fastest-growing demographic in small business start-ups and entrepreneurships.

In early 2021, I closed the loop on the framework with the Inclusive Business Retreat, which I adapted from my initial one-off consultations with clients to provide them with anti-racism and anti-oppressive plans and recommendations for their life and business.

Over a period of two years I developed a framework consisting of six video classes totalling over twelve hours of content, and six PDF workbooks.

One of the hardest things for most humans is looking at ourselves when we make a mistake or hurt someone.

Diverse communities

At a wedding in 2005, I was asked the question 'what breed are you?' by a pale, stale, male. As if my appearance was inferior and that I could be reduced to a breed of an animal, unlike his white self. The inflection that I was a mongrel was apparent to me. It was the first time in years that anyone spoke to me in such a revoltingly racist way. The question is inexcusable whether alcohol was involved or not. Racism is deeply ingrained in people no matter their sobriety, no matter their 'but I'm not a racist' statements.

It's not my job as a biracial person to pardon or provide emotional labour to people like that man, nor is it the job of any melanated and racialised person. I was so shocked by the question and the insulting tone that instead of telling him to GTFO of my face, I answered him as though he spoke to me with courtesy. He didn't deserve my polite response. He didn't deserve my time. He didn't deserve my presence.

I have been asked where I am from and what my background is more times than I can remember. It seems the question is an acceptable entry point into conversations with every stranger I meet. After forty years I am sick of the question and now refuse to answer it. I am a person, and I am no less Australian. I have a right to be here.

I relate to much of what Arden Cho shares in her *What am I?* YouTube video and interview. I reference it in the hope that it serves to remind non-melanated and non-racialised people everywhere of their internalised racism and that curiosity is completely offensive, particularly if you are incapable of asking respectfully. My advice is don't ask and don't make it the first question you impose on another person. There is more than meets the eye and finally, not everything is your business to know.

As I joined more diverse communities talking and speaking about issues that matter to me, human rights, social justice, collective care unpacking and decolonising, I came across the term anti-racist. I didn't realise until I heard the term that it's something that I've always been, it's something that I've always shown up for. I guess you can't be in the body that I'm in and not be anti-racist.

You can of course have internalised racism and oppression, and part of your journey as a Person of Colour is to unravel all of that. So, my journey of becoming anti-racist began by wanting to have more genuine, broad conversations about the world and current affairs, life, politics and social justice, topics that I may have steered clear of in the past because I have to say, 'I'm not a fan of politics'. Becoming anti-racist meant I was already on the journey of unpacking my identity, before I claimed to become anti-racist.

I was looking at my identities. A lot of the spiritual modalities and communities I had been part of talked more about ancestral healing and ancestral trauma. And so, in going through those modalities and learning more about them and taking those journeys for that connection, I came to realise that was the journey that I was on. As I was unravelling, I was learning more about my identity. And the journey of identity is not an easy one. It's quite challenging, actually, because it has to undo over four decades of living.

I've had a lot of time to reflect on the experiences and encounters that I've had, the battles I've fought on a personal level, and dealing with individual racism to my face and in the social media space since I started writing and talking more about my beliefs over the last five years.

Human rights has always been a topic that I've written about, maybe not as extensively as creativity; I wrote about creativity and art very early on. Since I started writing online, I expected that I would also write about the political climate, current affairs, social justice and human rights issues because we can't ignore these things; they're in our face, but it is easy for the most privileged to bypass these topics because they don't experience these issues in daily life. They are usually the perpetrators of the behaviour that we as marginalised people experience daily, which requires us to do so much more learning so that we can decode all of the lies, conditioning biases and stereotypes that have been thrust upon us without our permission.

My journey of identity is one of finding myself and getting to define me for myself. It's such a journey of sovereignty and finding that within myself, and being able to express myself through writing. Lastly, becoming anti-racist has been tremendously healing while very confronting and terrifying at times.

It's caused me to grow ever more discerning, to develop much stronger boundaries, and not only boundaries with others but with boundaries with myself because I'm someone who cares about others and wants others to do better.

A lot of that involves me putting myself out there in a way that has been vulnerable and uncomfortable at times, and what I've learned from this is that the most work that we can do, whether it is on a personal level or in the way that we show up in our businesses, is really that of inner self-awareness. And this is why self-awareness is the first class in my Unpack Your Privilege course and the anti-racist and anti-oppression learning framework that I first conceptualised in 2017, before teaching it in 2018. The journey to put together Unpack Your Privilege did not start on a positive note. I think about all of the other reasons for becoming an artist, for becoming a writer, for becoming fully expressed, for becoming healed, for reclaiming the pursuit of wholeness and betterment.

I want to have a better life, I deserve a better life and I want to see where this road takes me. The journey to becoming anti-racist began with my love and passion for human rights, justice for all and doing what's right. What hit the accelerator on becoming anti-racist was racism from white family members. Now, this is not terribly uncommon. Those of us who are mixed race or biracial with white family members know what this is like and how triggering and painful and traumatising this is, so I want to start with a warning to take care of yourself as you read this chapter, if you relate to my identities or if you hold marginalised identities yourself.

I was so shocked to discover family members' outward racism towards me, and microaggressions when I used the term white supremacy in a private post I wrote on my personal Facebook page. As I touched on before, that's where this really all began. Now I know this work is worth it. I must do it now. I know that this is part of my purpose because I'm not going to let it go after all of this personal healing and spiritual growth work. There is no way that I'm going to let family members make me feel less than or have me experience the same triggers and racial traumas that I have encountered through my entire life.

I've already talked about how I am estranged from the 'family' that I experienced racism from. I have had no contact with them in over three years. It caused me a lot of pain and grief in the initial aftermath, knowing that they were people who had backed me and supported me, those who I'd grown close to despite living on the other side of the world.

And I just couldn't get past the fact that they felt it was okay to tell me that I was being stupid and ridiculous and it's nonsense that white supremacy exists, only to read some months later that in a neighbouring county there were white supremacists in action not far from where they lived.

And while that gave me a certain sense of satisfaction, I was still experiencing the pain, grief and loss of being personally harmed by members of my family, my blood kin, from whom I had expected better. This is the thing about expectations in this work. We need to dispense with the expectation that people who say they love us, who showed up for us previously, who are related to us, who are a part of our family, whether that's blood or soul family, are for us. We can't be guaranteed that the more we dive into becoming anti-racist, no matter what our identities are, that there aren't people close to us already who are going to be incredibly uncomfortable with the path that we are taking. There will be discomfort felt around the conversations that we are starting to have and all the interruptions when we hear them say racist or phobic things.

There's a lot to be said for the phrase 'benefit of the doubt' that we grant almost instantly to people. We try to acknowledge their good intentions or make excuses for them because they didn't mean what they said, they don't have the knowledge or education to know it was wrong, but we already know through several hundred years of colonisation, xenophobia and genocide that racism exists. This is an undeniable fact, and to be told by people with more privilege that racism and white supremacy don't exist is basically a spit in the face to your identity and all the ways in which you are different from them.

I don't grant people the benefit of the doubt anymore because I'm more concerned about the prioritisation of heart over harm and impact over intention. For me, these are two phrases that work together. Other people write about impact over intention and in the development of my class, racial trauma, awareness, privilege and harm are inextricably linked.

That's where I came up with heart over harm: bringing our compassion, bringing our heart, bringing our empathy and prioritising kindness and gentleness over blurting out things that might hurt or harm other people. This is the core of my work; love is at the heart of my teachings.

These are things that I look at when I'm thinking about or experiencing racism. We've been conditioned by society to give people the benefit of the doubt, to put forth whataboutisms and to really focus on the belief that everyone is inherently good when we know that is simply not true. And I know I sound jaded, and that might make people feel uncomfortable, but I can only speak from my own experiences and my truth. More often than not, my wariness about giving someone the benefit of the doubt has not been misplaced.

Becoming anti-racist has demanded that I capitalise on my resilience, the resilience that I gained from multiple life experiences that have been challenging and traumatising and difficult. This has unfortunately meant tapping into survival mode: the mode that has us doing what we can to protect ourselves. And besides, it's not pleasant being hypervigilant twenty-four-seven. It's not pleasant being suspicious or distrusting of others, but as I've explained, we already know that sometimes our hearts and our bodies aren't safe in our own homes or in the homes of our families and friends when we're undertaking a journey of anti-racism.

I find it really interesting that people look at anti-racism as something to learn. They see it as a challenging undertaking. I'm not sure what that's about. There's the discomfort, the fact that if I put it into the framing of a spiritual and healing journey is not easy and can be quite uncomfortable. I'm wondering why people cannot come to the education on anti-racism, knowing that, yes, it's going to be uncomfortable, but what you will learn will be worth it because it means that you will become a better human and you will limit hurt or harm others.

I think the biggest challenge that privileged people in particular face when it comes to becoming anti-racist is the very close examination of yourself that you are required to do when you are becoming self-aware, to unpack your identities and unpack all of the ways that you have benefited from systems of oppression, the ways you've been complicit with silence and the ways you've been appropriating and profiting from cultures that are not your own. When you live on stolen land, or when you come from a nation that colonises, it is your duty as a good human being to become anti-racist. It's something that everyone should become.

While I want to dispense with the use of using, you know, 'don't do this', 'don't do that', 'you shouldn't do this', 'you shouldn't do that'. I do want to say that becoming anti-racist benefits all of us. It benefits if you are a privileged person and you're in a privileged body. You just haven't seen a world where systems of oppression don't exist yet. And neither have I. But, sure, I would fucking love to see a world where white supremacy and systems of oppression are dismantled, a society where we have genuine equity. I would love to see what that would look like. And right now all I can do is dream it, imagine it and do what I can in my work, even if I don't get to see the outcome in trying to make things better for people like myself and people who are more marginalised. To me, that's an important priority.

There's no saviourism in just wanting to do better and acknowledging that the world has the resources to sustain everyone. Yet, we are seeing people who have obscene amounts of privilege and wealth behaving like the kid who doesn't want to share their crayons. It's childish but it is also highly manipulative and intentional.

REFLECTION
QUESTIONS

If you've experienced anything similar to what I've documented in this chapter. I'm so sorry. I wish much better for you.

- What action can you take today to heal from painful experiences about your identities?
- What boundaries can you raise?

For everyone else:

- Dive into your privilege, social identities, beliefs, biases, behaviours and stereotypes. What are they?
- What lessons can you take away from this chapter?
- What action can you take to become anti-racist and inclusive?

13
Purposeful

A wise teacher does not ask you to enter the house of his wisdom,
but rather leads you to the threshold of your mind.'
—Kahlil Gibran

So much potential

All through my working life, I've been in conversations with employers about my 'potential', about them seeing my potential while I remained clueless for years about what they meant. Do I have some invisible Castiel-like silhouetted wings only they can see? Looking back, my cluelessness was really more a lack of communication on their part and as an autistic person and a person with ADHD, I need more upfront information, because reading between the lines of what people say takes me to overthinker central. I wasn't equipped back then to ask, 'What potential? What do you mean?'. This set me off on a wild path of self-discovery to unpack my potential and my purpose, whatever the hell that was! I was like a hobbit on a quest.

My quiet nature and shyness was overt, and I had difficulty speaking up and raising my voice enough to be heard unless there was something to fight for. I look back and I was such a different version of myself then. Quite a wallflower and often described as one. It was a description that stuck for a long time.

One of my fondest work memories came about in 2000 when I applied for a job with a now-closed IT&T executive search firm, acronym O.C. I was recruited as their administration person. I worked there for eighteen months before our office was closed and we were made redundant. Up until that point, it was the best job I'd ever had, and today, it is still up there as one of the best, alongside my current employment. As a twenty-three year old in this new work environment, I was supported beyond my expectations. I felt like I belonged, and I did. The managing director scheduled one-on-one meetings with me every month to mentor and support me. It was my first experience of being mentored and coached, and most certainly one of the best coaching experiences I have ever had, because it wasn't about changing me or how I did things but supporting me to be more of who I was and to bring more of 'me' out. I am so grateful I had this experience early on. Without knowing it, it was really the start of self-acceptance for me. This working experience did set a very high benchmark that unfortunately went unmatched for decades.

The sessions with the managing director and time spent working with the business partners and consultants helped to bring me out of my shell. I was given more responsibility and became a valued member of the team. We socialised outside of work and this connection deepened our working relationships. I received lots of positive feedback, encouragement and recognition from the consultants I worked with. I can see now how I helped them just as much as they helped me, not just with our assigned duties and responsibilities, but as humans working together and supporting one another.

Working in a positive work environment at that age had a huge impact on my confidence and abilities. My confidence grew and I began to feel like I could speak up, offer my opinions, thoughts and ideas because they were requested, validated and appreciated. This environment taught me what it meant to be part of a team, and that I could be part of one and be seen. I never felt particularly confident before; I didn't give it too much thought until much later. Working with people can make or break you. I certainly found that with jobs that came thereafter. People make a difference and finding great people and a great working environment is rare.

As a dot connector who recognises patterns easily, the one thing this and my current workplace have in common is that they were/are people focused and people centred. The first, helping others to find suitable employment in the IT&T field, and the current, helping and caring for the health and wellbeing of people by providing essential services that enable independence, quality of life, community engagement, improved wellbeing and health outcomes, and more, while also supporting and caring for the staff that undertake the work.

Mindset and outlook

I'm not going to tell you to change your 'mindset'. I hate that word and the shallow way it which it is often used in the online marketing streets.

I've thought about this for a long time and haven't found the words until now. This is my opinion based on an open-minded, broad world view that has involved me healing and peeling back a lot of trauma layers and doing, creating and practising deep, transformative, life-changing coaching work that my inclusive long-term clients and leaders love.

I'm going to work with you to deepen your self-awareness and support you to reframe your outlook of yourself and the world we live in.

'Mindset' is a fucked-up word because of the way it has been used, weaponised and featured in persuasive and manipulative marketing tactics. This is often devoid of any self-awareness or acknowledgement of white privilege from the user, and it then gets used by people in the margins who consume that content.

I'm a writer and award-winning coach doing things differently.

If you'd like to shift and transform beyond the binary, beyond the capitalist BS, and receive deep, personal and professional coaching, education and support that'll help you move through the world with a feminist, anti-racist and anti-oppressive lens and outlook, I'm the inclusive human for you.

Gutsy Soul Note: dream-making is essential

This Gutsy Soul Note came through me a few days ago: dream-making IS essential.

The dream means something. The dream is worth the blood, sweat and tears. The dream is about taking every chance and not sitting at the sidelines being too afraid to try. The dream was built from the ground up by me. The dream is about living life to the fullest and not getting to my deathbed and regretting what I didn't do. Your dreams do not have to look like someone else's, they don't have to be conventional, they don't have to include the corporate cubicle (unless that's what you want), they don't have to follow a straight line. Don't be disheartened when those who love you don't get it, they don't have to. It's YOU who has to be into you, into your work, passions, dreams, magic.

I craved to be understood. It took a long time to not seek that in the wrong places. I've learned through these five years of Gutsy Girl in her many transformations (mixed media art, handmade silver jewellery, blogging, writing, women's circles, workshops, online courses) that it's not *really* important to be understood by everyone. I don't have to be understood by my loved ones at all. So long as I believe in what I'm doing, I can find kindred spirits along the way who have their own passions, who 'get it', and we can cheer, support, encourage and inspire each other.

REFLECTION
QUESTIONS

- What dream will you commit to starting?
- What promises will you make to yourself to keep you following your dreams no matter what?
- What are your values, mission and manifesto for chasing your dreams with fervour?

One thing I know: The world needs you doing your thing and living your potential—on your terms.

It's oh so quiet

I got afraid when my income went deadly quiet for a few months in early 2020. I applied for a dozen jobs I didn't want. It was a drain on my energy, and I felt under-resourced to be applying for jobs while trying to grow my business. Every role I applied for I wasn't even considered for, and these were roles that asked for five-plus years of experience in positions where I had fifteen years.

The universe was telling me that what I was doing was out of alignment with my future direction—whatever the hell that was. I stopped applying for jobs, going against the well-meaning advice and concern of loved ones, and decided I'd blaze my own trail even if it meant I had to struggle for a time to get where I wanted to go with the path I had chosen. I had to believe in myself and take a chance and keep going no matter what. I couldn't allow the concern or fears of others to influence my decision making.

What did I learn from this?

Nobody knows me better than I do. Mistakes or misdirections are mine to make. Nobody doling out the advice had ever done what I was doing or created anything from scratch as I was doing, so trusting my intuition and being guided by soul and spirit became a new practice.

I was still uncertain and afraid. Terrified, if I'm honest. It isn't easy to practise something new and unfamiliar in the face of obstacles, challenges and other people's opinions. I'm still learning to make this way of being a habit.

Learning to catch myself at every stumble, fall or crash of self-confidence and self-belief that I was still in the very early days of developing.

It's an ironic thing to be forty-two (at that time) and still finding my way to confidence. I'd never felt confident until I started Gutsy Girl in 2012, embracing my artistry and creativity, and then starting Formidable Voices in 2019 and embracing self-expression and stepping into event creator, host and speaker.

Stopping yourself from allowing other people's fear to control your actions is a practice. It takes time. Please be kind and gentle with yourself.

Communicating boundaries and holding steadfast to being the best person to yourself.

The story of the incredible shrinking desk

A while back, I ended up working with someone who caused me extreme distress. I had been with the company for five years at this stage and he started as my manager. He refused to use the electronic and secure systems we had and treated me like his personal admin assistant even though I was a contracts specialist. He gaslit me and fucked with my insecurities and I ended up with work-related PTSD on top of existing PTSD due to past trauma. The story is much like the diagram The 'Problem' Woman of Colour in the Workplace by the Safehouse Progressive Alliance for Non-Violence.[3]

During this absolutely shit time, I was plagued with insomnia, my period stopped and took over six months to return after I was demoted via PowerPoint and transferred to another division following my complaint about his bullying behaviour.

I, the Woman of Colour (as I identified myself at the time) was punished for daring to challenge the white male. Due to space constraints as the business grew, I had to share a one-person office with this man. It was the most unpleasant working environment in my twenty-four-year corporate career. No one would come into the shared office to speak with me because they disliked him immensely.

An invisible storm cloud formed above me, and my whole personality and happy nature disappeared. I had the black dog. Again. I lost time with my sweet girl and husband, with weekends spent exhausted in bed trying to recover from the past week and trying to muster up the energy for the week ahead.

My time and soul were stolen by this arsehole like a rotten little tooth fairy who leaves no coins. Every single day I dreamt about getting the fuck out of there never to return. I called that little office we shared 'my departure lounge'. My side gig was blogging, mixed media art, jewellery making, women's circles and workshops. It was early days, and there was no time to grow the side gig, nor did I have the capacity with dwindling mental health to seek employment elsewhere. When I was able to sleep (due to an excess of red wine, a bad habit that was a crutch for several months), I had bizarre dreams, one of which was the incredible shrinking desk.

In this dream, I would come to work and each day, what was supposed to be my desk would be located in another part of the building away from people I worked with (including him—so, a dream only). The desk would shrink in size every day, and I'd have a 'WTF?! is going on' moment every single time. I was like a biracial Alice with a large potion bottle of red wine labelled 'drink me' and a shrinking desk I could barely sit at. Eventually, the desk would become non-existent, and I grew more curious about what the hell this dream meant and if it was a prophecy of some kind.

It turns out some three years later I was made redundant because the company realised after a restructure that forcing me to return to work with him would be an unethical move on their part. Particularly as a year prior they re-traumatised me by having me support his workload (when the person who replaced me left after her bullying experiences with him) and he crossed a working boundary with me by 1) speaking to me, and 2) being a manipulative creep trying to get me to do more work than what was agreed in writing.

This experience also changed many things, from how I set and enforce boundaries, how I use my voice and how I speak up even when I know what I have to say is not going to be well received. I am that person in the diagram. I was until I made the best of being cast out by rocking my coaching and consulting business, writing my heart out, creating nine online classes, four group coaching programs, multiple guest teaching opportunities and creating Formidable Voices over two years.

All that I've created I would have eventually done over time. I don't subscribe to the idea that the pain and psychological injury I endured at my former workplace made me a better, stronger person. I was already strong. I was already kind and compassionate, and that could not be taken from me. This did not happen 'for a reason'. It happened because the man was an arsehole. I had to deal with him and other non-racialised and non-melanated people who did not give a fuck about my mental health. My successful performance was diminished. Prior to him, I was doing solo contract work and carrying the entire division for several months. That experience fucking broke parts of me. It also caused me to do the work of anti-racism, anti-oppression and anti-bias now. I believed the lie that whiteness tells people and Women of Colour in the workplace that being mistreated is down to a 'communication issue'. That's code for: you are wrong and how dare you question white authority and be 'too sensitive'. Instead of apportioning accountability to the toxic, sexist, manipulative, abusive, gaslighting white male bully who cut me down every day at every opportunity. I had to endure working with him for six months. My confidentiality was breached by another, and they also revealed my anxiety to him. Another person I approached broke my trust and minimised my concerns when I raised them, did not speak to me again and could not hold my gaze if our eyes met, so I would give him a death stare every time I saw him for those final years. My death stare is pretty withering, so I'm told.

I've been repairing and healing and ascending ever since I left that workplace. I'm attempting to build an international business that gives me freedom, pays the bills and supports my family. To the patriarchy, those people I worked with who caused me extreme distress, I raise both my middle fingers.

If you are a racialised and melanated person, or if you relate to my story and are dreaming of your incredible shrinking desk, I want you to know four things:

1. You are an incredible human;
2. You can create and innovate like no one else;
3. You are BEYOND worthy of respect, justice, ethical and professional conduct, and to be believed and listened to when you raise a matter of concern;
4. I believe in you, and you have what it takes to do whatever you set your mind and heart on.

14
Formidable Voices

'Be yourself until you make them uncomfortable.'
—Alok Vaid-Menon

Gender, pronouns and becoming self-defined

Throughout this book you may have noticed me switching the pronouns I use to describe myself as I tell my story. Long before my awareness and education about pronouns and gender identity, I referred to myself as she/her. For the past few years, my pronouns have been she/they. If you refer to me by pronouns, I prefer they/she at the time of writing this chapter. I would rather you speak my name and refer to me by my name.

I am a human. 'Woman' is too small a description for how I describe myself today. It doesn't encompass my entire being to the extent that 'human' does. To describe myself as 'woman' today reduces my personhood. I am beyond definition. This is not ego talking, that's the truth. I cannot and refuse to be contained by one socially constructed descriptor. I am more than an assigned gender, assumed gender, more than just some woman and girl who was sexually assaulted, physically assaulted, emotionally manipulated, cheated on and abused, and bullied and harassed in the workplace. I define myself. My definition of myself and how I describe myself is not up for debate, discussion, critique or opinion. I am sovereign. I decide the labels I assume and nobody else gets to do that on my behalf, ever. I have boundaries. I know my mind, my body, my identities, my magic, my purpose, my soul work, my passions. Once I knew all of this, I dropped the need for validation and the craving to be liked by anyone because I am not for just anyone or everyone.

The back and forth of becoming

There are many stories I've started and lived over the past decade of sovereign self-exploration. I discovered through more than twenty-seven canvases, countless journal and sketchbook pages and sheets of mixed media and watercolour paper that art saves me when I need deep healing, when I'm consumed with grief and unravelling and untangling from the wild ride of life, all the while bringing me ever closer to a place of wholeness and integration.

I don't use the words lightly when I say that when I get to my deathbed, I want to have done everything possible to live every bit of my life to its fullest—no regrets. When the last breath comes, I want it to be the deepest, most peace-filled exhale of all.

I want to share with you my transformative journey from being a daydreamer to a writer who has not only created but lived the stories I tell. As I grew up, I realised I had the wildest, biggest imagination and dreamscapes to draw from and I often thought that I would someday end up becoming a writer of fiction. I made some murmurings towards that back in 2008 when I enrolled in an online creative writing short story course with the view to focus on fiction.

As I've been reminded by a lifetime of stories, dreams, visions and experiences over the years, I've identified that the lines between reality and my dreams have blurred quite a lot. Different brain. Life through my lens is not just this plane I live on, but I live many more through my dreams and visions and endless daydreaming. Many worlds, characters, roles and plots in my head, but none come out as a silver thread that fits into a vial. No, the stories I get to tell, at least for now, are the ones I've lived, the paths I've crossed, the many yeses, the noes, the risks and leaps. So many leaps. I'm a Life Path 7, the seeker, the teacher. A lamp post in the dark. A cliff from which I leap again and again.

Before we moved from my hometown of Sydney to Brisbane in 2010, just as our daughter turned four years old, I returned to exploring art. This included drawing classes, crafting jewellery, creating abstract art explorations at home and experimental drawing on Saturdays at Brett Whiteley's studio. I got back into it because I wanted to play, have fun, experiment and see what these canvases, paper and art materials could draw from me.

After we moved to Brisbane, I took a few different routes of self-discovery on my way back to art. I joined a trapeze arts class and a hula hooping class which I went to after work.

I found art journaling classes online when I was considering making a scrapbook. I joined classes and communities and excavated so much of myself and painted my heart out. I returned to making jewellery again and began my first blog in 2012. Putting myself out there was no easy feat.

An encounter with a fellow creative at my daughter's school lead me to ramp up my creative side-gig efforts, and I joined BrisStyle and applied for a stall at the Christmas markets. For nine weeks, I made lots of things for the market. I also set up my store on Etsy. Things were moving very fast as I dived into creativity to replace my social life. Finding friends and likeminded people took a hell of a lot longer than expected, and instead of Brisbane, I found most friendships with people in different time zones and countries.

I discovered I liked talking about creativity and my creations with people who came by my market stall. I continued to do market stalls for five years until I became fully online with my gift box store and shifted to workshops: circles in 2015 and online programs in 2016.

I took more online art classes, more for community than anything else, because I enjoyed experimenting and making art my way.

Through connections in an online art community, I joined an art collaborative in 2013. We created a collaborative mixed media art piece and held an art exhibition of our own in Paddington, Brisbane. It was a huge undertaking as I continued to paint whenever I could to bring a small collection of artworks together. I showcased acrylic, mixed media, oil and cold wax creations on wood and a couple of my jewellery pieces. It felt really courageous to do this and while the rewards weren't monetary, the process of healing I went through during that period is beyond compare. Time would tell just how much. It was some years ahead before the total untangling and unravelling happened.

In 2019, after four house moves in nine years, it was time to surrender that which I'd held onto. We piled our clutter into the back of our car, including my twenty-seven canvases layered in paint and ink, colourful and intense yet incomplete. I watched as I tossed them into the pit—letting go of the wounds—those paintings soothed and healed to rebuild and bring to life new skin. As I cast them over the edge, little pieces of my soul sprouted. Like the light edging over a shadow in the sunlight, I felt a physical burden fall away from my shoulders. I don't have to carry these wounds this way any longer. I give myself permission to be free of what I faced and relived and soothed the edges of with paint, oil and tunes. The cloying scent of rubbish and debris awaiting its final crushing by a bulldozer. Many dreams, spells, wishes and words—banishing and releasing—were scrawled beneath the paint of those canvases. And now, unburdened, I dreamt of what it would be like to feel free. Liberated. Artful and eternally joy filled. I guess it was time to find out.

Going solo

At the time of writing this chapter, it's March 2021 and I'm on my solo writing retreat on Wangerriburra land, also known as the Valley of the Owls. Full stop. I carved out four days in my schedule because I could tell that if I was just going to stay at home to write this chapter,

I could not write the best chapter possible. I had to be immersed in the process. I wanted to give this chapter the best possible energy and attention because for starters, we need to see more melanated and racialised writers with books published and on bookshelves.

It's been my longest dream to not only be a writer, but to also become an author, and it was this dream that I held so close to my chest for so long that no one actually knew about it until three or four years ago. I never told anyone that this was my biggest dream, which says a lot about why self-belief is so important because I didn't want to put it out into the world that I wanted to write a book or become an author in case it didn't happen. If I voiced it, then it would mean that people would constantly ask me how the book was going. I didn't need the added pressure, so when I first began writing a book in 2017, no one really knew about it. I've held this dream very close to my chest all this time.

I began by putting together all my writing from various places, from my former blog to where I bared my soul in my Google Docs and other writing that I had jotted down in the Notes app on my phone. It was all these writings that formed the basis of this book. And just to be clear, this book is not the one I first set out to write. This book is the transformation, the shapeshifter version of the book that I intended to write once I learned the many lessons that are contained in this book.

So, my journey to becoming an author has been going for quite some time. I'm forty-four years old. And as I sit here in this cute little cottage on retreat right now, I'm still in somewhat disbelief that I have a publishing contract with the kind press.

I was honoured to be the recipient of The Spirit Scholarship, a partnership between the kind press and Beautiful You Coaching Academy, where I trained to become a qualified coach.

Five days ago, I was the recipient of the Beautiful You Coaching Academy 2020-2021 Emerging Coach of the Year. I still cannot believe that this level of recognition is happening. And I have to say, there has been a shift in me in the last few days.

There's a shift in my perception of self, my self-belief and confidence. I feel more confident to use my voice and show up on video than I have done previously. I've spoken about having visibility fears for a few years now. As I have been writing this book and going through notes and writings and journals from the last eight years, it's interesting to see that. It really does require a daily practice to believe in ourselves.

This is not about 'manifesting' your biggest dream or believing so hard that something is going to happen that it does happen, becoming an author has taken work; it's taken a lot of exposure, vulnerability, tears, heart sharing, hurting and reclusiveness to build up the courage to write my story.

I've nurtured this baby for a very long time.

When I was fourteen years old, probably when the thought first popped into my head about writing and wanting to become an author, it was a time where I was reading a lot of books, because we had to for school, but also because I really enjoy reading and I love immersing myself in a story. I loved to escape to new worlds, other places, different timelines, different characters. And while for many years books have served to be a place of escaping reality, they are also a place that can help us build and grow our dreams.

Books have been a safe haven for me to dream big and imagine possibilities. I found them within the pages of a book as a small child. I recall living in a little ground floor unit that my parents and I lived in until I was about eight years old. Through my very 1970s bright orange lattice-style curtains, my room would have this orange glow every morning at first light. I would wind up my little blind just to catch a bit more light, and I would read. I remember this as far back as when I was at the age of reading Little Golden Books like *The Saggy Baggy Elephant* and *The Little Engine That Could*. I remember reading *The Saggy Baggy Elephant* a lot. I just love that story for so many reasons and I can still picture the illustrations so vividly in my mind.

When I was younger, I thought that the kind of book I would write would be like the books that I had read, full of adventures, new worlds, supernatural elements and abilities. I never believed that my story would be the story that I would go on to tell. But what I've learned over the years is how much I love the stories that we as humans tell one another, and I was sure there was something in it worth sharing.

My dad is such a wonderful storyteller. Upon reflection, I draw a lot of inspiration from him. As a small child, I could never get sick of his stories. As I grew, there was a point during my adolescence where I would say, 'Ah, not this story again'. But now that I'm in my forties, I want to hear all those stories again. He was a young man who travelled solo by ship to Australia after having left his homeland of Northern Ireland at age sixteen. My dad's storytelling never misses a beat. If you are curious about the power of story but cannot fathom its depths, I say this: when my dad and I speak and old names and places come up, his memories are just beneath the surface. I can hear the joy of memory, story, experience, adventure and wisdom in his voice depending on what story he is about to tell. Each of us is adventurous in our own way. If I'm to be guided by an example of a human who has experienced life, adventure and the persistence of memory and powerful, enticing storytelling, I can't think of anyone better as a personal influence.

Story shares the root of my creations

In 2019, after three years of daydreaming about it and holding the vision and the radiance of it, I announced Formidable Voices initially as an online community, off social media, before the daydream part came into being. I was launching and creating a speaking event of racialised and melanated women living in Australia and abroad from many cultural backgrounds. I was so bored and sick of the whitewashed panels and line-ups of speakers in events covering coaching, leadership, spirituality, wellness and empowerment. What was there for us who weren't the default (i.e., white)?

What drove me to create Formidable Voices came from the question: what are we all missing out on when we don't see diverse and equitable representation in our industries?

What expertise, experience, nuances and wisdom are you missing out on? There are a WEALTH of incredible humans with amazing work that we just aren't getting exposed to because of the same old, same old ways of leadership and who gets a seat at the table.

Looking back at every event I had been to up until this point, I was not shocked to notice that all were far from inclusive, diverse and equitable. How on earth could hearing the same message delivered slightly differently by people who shared the same privilege, identities, access and who get invited constantly, teach me how to empower myself, with all my diverse and divergent identities, and apply their teachings to my life? I tried, and the results were negligible. I can see now that I didn't grant myself the level of grace, respect and worthiness I deserved.

It was time for Formidable Voices to be considered first, not as an afterthought or checkbox strategy to tokenistic inclusion and diversity. Formidable Voices was necessary to alter the landscape just slightly so people could experience our brilliance and notice for themselves what a speaker line-up could be like if the table and space was built for us. The strength of my community and connection with others meant that I could collaborate and bring together a wonderful line-up of people from near and far and partner with aligned sponsors who supported the event. Formidable Voices became an events, online membership space and movement that centred on the stories and voices of Black, Indigenous and Women of Colour that year.

The global events and membership community welcomed people from many industries and professions to support and attend our first event. Among the community were leaders, entrepreneurs, activists, advocates, consultants, life coaches, business coaches, authors, writers, speakers, teachers, small business owners, creatives, artists, makers, publishers, graphic illustrators, healing and spiritual practitioners, priestesses, sacred circle leaders, astrologers and brujas.

I made it the mission of Formidable Voices events to aid those willing to bring forth all their gifts, to express their message and be forces of good in the world. With Formidable Voices, I strove to deliver, highlight, enhance and uplift incredible, underrepresented voices and leaders of colour across multiple platforms: coaching, creative, tech and online businesses, activism and social justice including speakers, writers, coaches, podcasters, published authors and healing modality practitioners and pioneers.

Formidable Voices welcomed people of all genders, along with accomplices, people who believed in a movement to focalise racialised, melanated and marginalised voices. Accomplices are people who are dismantling white supremacy and doing the transformative inner work to be forces of good in the world.

It was incredible to gather these brilliant people who had powerful stories to tell and showed immense presence when on the mic. The event was held in Melbourne in November 2019 to an audience of over sixty people. The speaker line-up was an absolute dream for me: Sonali Fiske, Jade McKenzie, Yolanda Finette, Anna Stassen, LJ Sparrey, Sora Schilling and yours truly. Sonali, Jade, Yolanda and I delivered keynotes, and I had a collaborative conversation with Anna and LJ about Reiki, being biracial and creativity. It was amazing to meet in person for the first time and converse with many peers and friends from afar who travelled to attend our event. I knew this was something I wanted to do again.

Soon after, the pandemic made travel and many things impossible, so a year later, I created Beam Your Brilliance, a virtual conference spanning ten days of roundtables, interviews and conversations. In a virtual setting it is possible to go bigger and better, so this line-up for the second Formidable Voices event grew to over twenty speakers from five countries and many diverse cultural backgrounds, including the original Formidable Voices speakers: Sonali Fiske, Jade McKenzie, Yolanda Finette, Anna Stassen, LJ Sparrey and Sora Schilling, as well as Lena West, Staci Jordan Shelton, Nisha Moodley, McKensie Mack, Ruby Hamad, Anuradha Kowtha, Mikael Egan, Jolinda Johnson, Asha Frost, Courtney Napier, Metzli Alexandria, Michelle Nicole, Tiffany Wong, Karen Larbi, Kundan Chhabra and Navi Gill.

It was an intense ten-day event and one I would only attempt in future with admin assistance. I coordinated and emailed all the speakers and event registrants as well as hosted up to three hours of conversations each day. It was amazing, rewarding and necessary but I don't think I would undertake an event of that size again unless I had a team to help perform every aspect required for launching, promoting, hosting and running an event. Over 200 people signed up with two dozen people taking up the buy one, gift one option to enable more racialised, marginalised and melanated people to attend the event.

In creating Formidable Voices and two events so far, I've learned that no matter the obstacles we face in transforming and growing ourselves, trying to be seen and heard and taking up space in all our brilliance, we must take a risk, a chance, and believe in ourselves to be able to create more beauty in the world that we want to experience and see. It's up to us to light up the world, claim and reclaim our rightful place and speak up in the face of denial, silence, inequity and underrepresentation. We don't have to do it alone, we do so as a village, in our community, and with generosity and courage in our hearts.

REFLECTION
QUESTIONS

- Define yourself for yourself.
- What challenges you about others embracing their wholeness and accepting their identities?
- What challenges do you personally face in embracing your wholeness and identities? How can you pave the way for change?
- What drives you to create?
- What lessons have you been learning?
- What lessons are you integrating now?
- What would you love to create?

15
Becoming You

Illuminate the world, be a beacon of light

I will experience the depth and breadth of my growth this year.
Abundance is already on its way. My path is clear of all limitations,
barriers and obstacles. I will make it so. I will kick them in. My
innermost self feels it and knows it. Something is brewing; it's the
truth. Richness is already here in many forms. My vision illuminates
pathways for others. It's a slow burn of subtlety and blazing embers. It
can always be both at once. To show the light we must be the light and
carry it onward. I shine my light of hope, change and transformation.
I am steadfast in holding this vision. I embody potency and power. I
will welcome all who become inclusive by nature and practise heart
over harm.

I honour balance within myself, my work and my self-belief. I carry
a space for nuance, duality and genuine change. I don't have to just see

it to believe it, I become it and that flows in whatever way is necessary to disrupt and dismantle lies and manipulation. I trust in what guides me. I trust in myself. This I know.

Joy is not optional

It can't be said often enough: joy is not optional. Joy is essential to you. Full stop. No long explanation.

Joy is what I regard to be the woolly underlay of my life and stories shared here from childhood to middle age. My impactful intention is to always actively seek joy, well, perhaps not during the rest and nap times! What I create, I create with gusto. I cultivate joy, I plant it, I nurture it and I harvest it. The same with happy memories; laugh long, out loud and with belly side stitches. All of this enables me to hopefully help a few hearts along the way. As I typed the previous sentence, I somehow typed 'song' instead of 'along': 'song the way'. I guess that's what these stories with a soundtrack serve to do: song the way forward. With music as our companion as we take the wheel on this ride called life, we can persevere, break free, mobilise, embolden, enliven and express all of who we are, undoing and unknotting outdated conditioning. Learn to be enthralled by the joy of your becoming.

Commitment tests us all

No matter how much we are encouraged and supported, or the wealth of resources available, some of us will not take the next step. We feel unworthy or our lives are just too busy to even consider doing just one more thing for ourselves. We are all on unique pathways and we are all at different stages and it's totally okay to be scared, to not be ready and to be distrustful of what lies ahead. I think about how sad it would be if we were always being the roadblock or handbrake to our own joy, happiness and life purpose. My intention for this wild and precious life I have is to THRIVE, not just SURVIVE. It's an intention I reflect on for every person I cross paths with. Life isn't easy, but it can be joyful.

The moment you make a commitment to yourself, it is a soul-defining and empowering moment. It's also terrifying. The pathway for the awakened human is not for the fainthearted. I know what it means to be stretched, transformed and morphed in ways I never thought were possible. I have had good days, plenty of not-so-good days... BUT I have been held, supported, witnessed, encouraged and inspired. Some part of me believed it. I haven't had to do it all alone.

I have experienced this multiple times every year for years. Every time I step up, I feel the change. I get really, really uncomfortable. I sometimes feel like giving up. Every time I say yes to myself, something in me shifts and I'm never who I was the moment before, ever again. I have had shocking head-pounding migraines and growing pains every step of the way since I woke up to my omnipotential[4]. Each of us can choose how our adventure unfolds. Even in moments of solitude and distress, I have seen potential and endless possibility, not the silver lining, but what's real. I am positive about the future without exactly knowing why. I'm cool with that. I'm sometimes also not at all cool with that! Sometimes I wish I knew that things would get easier. But what fun would this epic journey on this rollercoaster of life be if we knew what was coming every time?

Years ago, I wrote my personal manifesto:

Be true to yourself, stand your ground, stay strong and do not give up.

These words have anchored me. I regroup, soak, clear, ground, breathe, pause, retreat, rest, dance, sing, cry, laugh—whatever it takes to get back on track. I keep trying in all kinds of ways even if I feel I've given up in others. I feel the wild truth in the shadows. I know that I'm becoming, and I know that when the time comes, I will see the brilliance in the lessons I'm learning.

Life has shown me that I can never be certain of what will set me off on a new path to deepen my experience, learning, awareness and understanding. When I'm presented with something new or make a discovery that could open up possibilities, deepen my life positively or negatively, I'm compelled to dive in and assess it.

Gutsy Leadership pillar

Fierce devotion is an act of self-compassion.

When you commit yourself fully to every lesson, life experience and teaching, you are loving yourself. You have made a decision to be here so commit to following through. Your ongoing commitment to yourself and your life purpose is a pure act of self-compassion and kindness. Ask yourself whether you are committed now and identify what you need to do to make self-compassion a daily practice.

My takeaway messages to you are:

You are more than enough.

Learn to have complete trust and faith in yourself. Get quiet, meditate, journal.

You have everything you need.

You don't have to know all the 'whys' if you feel drawn to doing something.

Be kind to yourself and give yourself time to grow, heal and flourish.

Pay attention to the signs and synchronicities.

Develop trust in the only voice that matters—your own.

REFLECTION
QUESTION

What do the Gutsy Leadership pillar takeaway messages above mean and feel to you? Define them for yourself.

Please rise

She told me no more.
This is the call.
No more self-doubt.
No more emotional beat ups about why it can't be you.
Whatever you want is ready for you to take.
The risk, the chance, is at your grasp.
Lean in and take it.
It takes guts, my darling.
But when you take that chance, you invest in you.
The unique masterpiece of your being, your soul.
You will harvest what you want and what you need.
I'd tell you take your time in another dimension, but we are in the here.
Where your dreams and all the answers you desire,
Reside.
Don't wait another second, a minute, an hour, a day, a week or a
month.
The voice within you says now is the time.
But I'm not ready, you reply.
Drink from the goblet of your desires,
You may never feel ready, but right now
all is at your feet.
You are who makes you whole.
No one else.
So many choices lay before you.
Trust that your heart knows what is right for you.
That is simply all it takes...
It can be this easy.

That's all she said. My inner voice. The one I quietened my whole life for fear of repercussions and anyone who told me that being as I am is too much for this world to take. So, I drank my desires in and embodied wholeness like never before.

Unravel and undo

I am limitless in potential but I'm not unlimited in my capacity, time or energy. I know I am. I've worked hard to unravel and undo all that I've been taught about being quiet, too much, not enough, too sensitive, too emotional, too opinionated, too feminist, too loud, too prudish, all the too-muchness that forms who I am.

When it comes down to it, all the traits that you get put down for are the traits that provide many of your best qualities. Your compassion, your introversion, your empathy, your lack of ego, your kindness, your generosity, your sensitivity, your desire to help, teach, support and encourage. The light and shadow are inextricably linked, and each requires the presence of the other. The fullness of me is needed. I need to show up in all my glory and all my mess. All my laughter and all my tears, which I often keep to myself. All my tirades and all my silences. All my soapbox sermons and hiding wallflower moments.

You are limitless in your own way. It is for you to see and believe in the beauty of you. Forget and leave those who want you to live a half-life. For it is not a life without all of your presence. We're waiting for you. You deserve to live more than a half-life. Don't wait. Unravel, undo and finally be you.

I am brave and courageous

It takes so much to live and take brave, courageous action. To step up and to keep going no matter how many battles, inner turmoil or obstacles are in our way. To not give up because the truth is only found within. To listen and trust our instincts, even if the decisions and choices we have to make terrify us, pulling us right out of our comfort zone into the space in between, the unknown and into the real dance with our shadow self. It can be truly exhausting, yet freeing, enlightening and re-energising too. I know that living and moving beyond the battles, diving deep into harnessing and owning my power, does lead to a more resilient self, one who overcomes obstacles and rises beyond. Whatever your battle or obstacle is, always remember that you are braver than you think.

In saying all of this, I'm shapeshifting once more. More out of tuning into my truth, my instincts and what genuinely feels good. Gutsy Girl has been many things since 2012, but she has never been boring to me! I came to a crossroads during and beyond battles and I have decided to allow my heart and soul to choose, and for what feels like the first time again (being a seeker and one whose purpose and presence here is always in transition), I'm fledgling with wings outstretched and taking yet another leap forward into the unknown with a sense of vitality I haven't felt in a long while. No more gripping to the 'comfort' of the jagged precipice.

It's time for metamorphosis and for a bigger vision to unfold. Returning to the true essence and spirit of your passions, your soul and the work you bring into the world. Take stock and become unstoppable, unbreakable and formidable.

REFLECTION
QUESTIONS

- What if everything is possible? Every dream, wish, intention, goal, plan, whisper?
- What if you were to say 'yes' and grant permission to be completely yourself?
- What brave decision will you make this week?
- What stirs within you that you've denied (revisit old stories, uncover the truth)?
- How close are you getting to who you really are (honour the journey so far, the stories and lessons along the way)?
- Will you leap, take a risk, be bold, make a courageous decision, deepen your self-belief and self-confidence?

You are in the midst of
your own becoming.

Epilogue

Once more, with feeling

As I begin to write the conclusion to this journey of becoming, I'm going through a few life transitions adjacently. I'm working at a not-for-profit in an environment and culture of prioritising people, offering health and wellbeing services, caring about our workforce, our communities and their wellbeing, a first in my working life which I am embracing with open arms.

We are looking for a new home and the rental market is dire, and the stress has been beyond overwhelming; migraines and meltdowns are frequent calendar events. I've been through storms in my life before and lived through them. I've been at a crossroads, having to make challenging choices, paths have opened up to new destinations and for now, I can see a small part of the road ahead. Much of it unknown, a mystery, a feeling of foreboding and immense hope for calmer seas, clarity of vision and a clear path without debris. I have been through trials and the internal battle of wills, and I can get through this again.

I remain undecided on the existence of reincarnation, but if life has taught me anything, we can burn things down, rebirth ourselves, make better choices, trust ourselves that little bit more, reclaim our joy and our stories, soothe what needs healing and recovery, find our centre once more and forge onward to rebuild anew. We are made of just *the* stuff.

I know more about myself today. With greater self-awareness comes responsibility to take this one life with both hands and live with joy, purpose and integrity. Recently discovering that I am autistic, have ADHD and hyper empathy has been an illuminating revelation. I feel very deeply and with gratitude, the times of elation, richness, joy, and deep love vastly add to my life, so when I do struggle, I am always tethered, anchored. I never sink.

The biggest revelation of my life somehow capped off a long list of 'No shit?!'. How did I or anyone not realise sooner? I can't help wishing the impossible wish that I had known this information earlier in my life, and if I had, how would that have changed my life? Would it have been easier or better? Would I have found wholeness and self-acceptance sooner? Would I have followed the breadcrumbs and listened to what path was being shown to me? That, we'll never know. But I know what's true, what's good and what brings more joy—and I'm going to dive deep into that.

I have faced changes, taken chances and had choices to make, and no matter where the road has taken me up to now, looking back, I've done what my life has required of me to get to the next destination and the one after that. It seems overly simple to figuratively say 'put one foot in front of the other' when life requires more of us than just our minds. Our life, the only life we may get, requires our hearts, our love, our compassion, our loyalty, our recognition of our interconnection with nature and all of life itself. Some parts of me, the ones that my mind computer hasn't figured out how to hack into, 'just know' and feel that I was called to this path I'm on and every challenge, obstacle and opportunity presented is just part of that calling. Maybe it's that I've thrown my hands up several times throughout my life asking, 'What the FUCK?'. I've existed being in a constant hypervigilant, anxious, hustle-like active state and learned the hard way that it is just not sustainable, it is barely survivable.

Now in my midlife, I've mellowed in some ways, grown confident in many others in ways I never thought possible, put some things to rest, become bolder and more outspoken from the quiet achiever of grade 6. I have definitely become more impatient and uncomfortable about transitions and change, but with a growing unwillingness to settle or accept the last resort or crumbs. I expect better. I work towards self-betterment and positive social change, my way.

Writing this book caused me to apply a magnifying glass to my life; I've been open, honest and vulnerable on these pages. I'm proud of who I am. I'm proud of my story, a story that is far from over. I used to feel that I had to show up all the time and feel discomfort, but I've untangled from that habit. It wasn't for me. Take enough time off social media and you'll realise how much your life is all the better for it. I am practising my boundaries. I am attempting to be kinder, slower and more patient with myself. My solitary time fills me up and fuels me up for the social engagements and work I choose to do. I'll equip myself with what I need to do things the way I want and how I want. The 'why' is always about more justice, joy, pleasure, love, healing and growing for everybody, without exception.

Being inclusive by nature is essential. I have choices and I leverage my privilege as much as I can. Using what I've got is important and it is for you in your life, too. We must ask ourselves: do we want to improve things for future generations, knowing we will never see the harvest of the hard work, perseverance and effort we put in? My answer has to be yes.

When I get to the end of my line, to my deathbed, I want to remember that I lived the second half of my life large, knowing I tried and did everything within my power to make it a good one, for it to be a life I lived once more, with feeling.

Writing this book has helped me make sense of so many things about myself and is an act of self-acceptance and love. But this too, is work.

I feel my special interest antennae twitching as I lock onto a new hobby: weaving. It makes a lot of sense, the circle from long before now to today, early winter 2022. I can still see the vibrancy of that red wool I used as a child to bind together ring pulls from cans to make bracelets. The markers my ma bought that we'd use for drawing and colouring in. The rolls of paper awaiting some magic from me. The circles I facilitated at first in-person and then online. All of this reminds me of my initial desire to become a handmade creative: I just want to make things. By extension, communities and spaces, too.

I'm at peace with my story and all the gory details. Self-reflection can be a bitch, but I sought out the lessons and meanings, and thanks to a daydreaming mind, I had the opportunity to redux. I'm looking ahead now, not backwards.

I can feel and remember every thread I've woven into and out of my life. Now as I approach my forty-sixth birthday, I feel more alive and grounded in myself. I wish this feeling could last. Thankfully, with memory, tethers, elation, joy and love at the core of this ever-living circle that is my one life, out loud: It is my hope that you free up your expression, explore, play and experiment with creativity and give yourself permission to ask yourself, why not me, why can't I be my own kind of gutsy and formidable?

I am still becoming.

The Soundtrack

'Music in the soul can be heard by the whole universe.'
—Lao Tzu

When I haven't had the words to express my feelings or process emotions, I've turned to music. Music has been a big influence in my life and provides me with inspiration for creativity, artistry, poetry, writing and passion. Beyond the music itself, the voices and lyrics, it's the feelings these tracks evoke within me that means the most. Combined, they add depth to my experience of life, my emotions and ability to process everything from pain to joy and euphoria.

The songs I've selected for this book are meaningful to me and you might just find something that wakes something up within you that will help you to put words to your emotions, feelings and life experiences.

I see these songs as complementing my story. Through reading my stories and listening to this music I hope they will aid and guide you into living with feeling and depth and support you to gain awareness, clarity and hopefully deepen or awaken a love for music, too.

'Disarm', The Smashing Pumpkins
'In Your Room', Depeche Mode
'Cloudbusting', Kate Bush
'Smells Like Teen Spirit', Nirvana
'Never Enough', The Cure
'Purple Haze', The Cure
'Buffalo Stance', Neneh Cherry
'Big Empty', Stone Temple Pilots
'Black Celebration', Depeche Mode
'Wave of Mutilation', Pixies
'Somewhere I Belong', Linkin Park
'Kiss', London After Midnight
'Ziggy Stardust', David Bowie
'She Sells Sanctuary', The Cult
'Fascination Street', The Cure
'Siren', Scarlet
'Freefall', The Tristan Chord
'Dance The Way I Feel', Ou Est le Swimming Pool
'Army of Me', Björk
'I Remember You', Skid Row
'Hunger Strike', Temple of the Dog
'Home', Depeche Mode
'Human Behaviour', Björk
'Peep Show', Miranda Sex Garden
'I Feel You', Depeche Mode
'Let Down', Dead by Sunrise
'Ruiner', Nine Inch Nails
'Coast Is Clear', Curve
'Birth Ritual', Soundgarden
'Crawling', Linkin Park
'Two Weeks', FKA twigs
'Cornflake Girl', Tori Amos
'Chloe Dancer/Crown of Thorns', Mother Love Bone
'Burn', The Cure
'Sour Times', Portishead

'Hey, Christian God', Snog
'Something I Can Never Have', Nine Inch Nails
'Pure Morning', Placebo
'Spider and the Fly', London After Midnight
'Fly', Miranda Sex Garden
'Come Undone', Duran Duran
'Hurt', Nine Inch Nails
'Sparks', Faith and the Muse
'Only Happy When It Rains', Garbage
'Obstacle I', Interpol
'Bizarre Love Triangle', New Order
'Stripped', Depeche Mode
'From the Edge of the Deep Green Sea', The Cure
'Temple of Love', Sisters of Mercy
'Cuts You Up', Peter Murphy
'Bachelorette', Björk
'Fade Into You', Mazzy Star
'You Look So Fine', Garbage
'Break & Enter', The Prodigy
'Breakdown', Joydop
'Fall To Pieces', Velvet Revolver
'Lying from You', Linkin Park
'Too Much', Kylie Minogue
'Control', Garbage
'Unfinished Sympathy', Massive Attack
'Hedonism (Just Because You Feel Good)', Skunk Anansie
'Brazen (Weep)', Skunk Anansie
'Not For You', Pearl Jam
'No More (This is the Last Time)', Depeche Mode
'The Becoming', Nine Inch Nails
'Walking in My Shoes', Depeche Mode
'In Your Room', Depeche Mode
'Out of the Blue', Funhouse
'Beautiful', Joydrop
'Freak Like Me', Sugababes

'Only When I Lose Myself', Depeche Mode
'Connection', Elastica
'One Hit to the Body', Suede
'Want', The Cure
'Crystal', New Order
'Violet', The Last Dance
'Rain', The Cult
'The Unforgettable Fire', U2
'Wild Horses', The Sundays
'Kool Thing', Sonic Youth
'Rooms on Fire', Stevie Nicks
'Malibu', Hole
'My Name Is Ruin', Gary Numan
'Second Skin', The Chameleons
'Policy of Truth', Depeche Mode
'Light Surrounding You', Evermore
'Sweet Disposition', The Temper Trap
'I am not a woman, I'm a god', Halsey
'1121', Halsey
'Big Jet Plane', Angus and Julia Stone
'Electric Feel', MGMT
'Goddess', BANKS
'New Romantics', Taylor Swift
'Yellow', Coldplay
'Plans', Birds of Tokyo
'The Real Thing', Faith No More
'As Heaven Is Wide', Garbage
'Need to Destroy', T.H.C.
'A Night Like This', The Cure
'Silent to the Dark', Electric Soft Parade
'Overfire', T.H.C.
'Drive', Incubus
'Came Back Haunted', Nine Inch Nails
'Safe From Harm', Massive Attack
'Rush', Depeche Mode

'Explode', Uh Huh Her
'Walls', Kings of Leon
'Runaways', The Killers
'Silence', Delirium (ft. Sarah McLachlan)
'Tear You Apart', She Wants Revenge
'Only Love Can Hurt Like This', Paloma Faith
'Aqueous Transmission', Incubus
'Apologize', OneRepublic
'Loneliest', Incubus
'Pendulum', Pearl Jam
'Way Down We Go', KALEO
'Rearviewmirror', Pearl Jam
'This Is What It Feels Like', BANKS
'Wake Up', Rage Against the Machine
'The Hand That Feeds', Nine Inch Nails
'Oh Bondage Up Yours!', X-Ray Spex
'Where's the Revolution', Depeche Mode
'Monster's Ball', Butcher Babies
'Up in Flames', Ruelle
'Paint It, Black', Ciara
'All of This and Nothing', Dave Gahan and Soulsavers
'Headstone', Djerv
'Cities In Dust', Siouxsie and the Banshees
'Halo', Depeche Mode
'Beggin for Thread', BANKS
'Castle', Halsey
'Illegal Attacks', Ian Brown (ft. Sinead O'Connor)
'Absolution Calling', Incubus
'Battle Symphony', Linkin Park
'Dog Days Are Over', Florence + The Machine
'Shine', Depeche Mode
'Halo', Beyonce
'Ocean', Goldfrapp (ft. Dave Gahan)
'Respect', Aretha Franklin
'Yes It's Fucking Political', Skunk Anansie

'Barracuda', Heart
'Sugar Water', Cibo Matto
'Superstar', Seeker Lover Keeper
'I'm No Angel', Dido
'Should Be Higher', Depeche Mode
'I Won't Back Down', Tom Petty
'Heads Will Roll', Yeah Yeah Yeahs
'Formation', Beyonce

Becoming you

'Enjoy the Silence', Depeche Mode
'Rome Wasn't Built ia Day', Morcheeba
'Be Yourself', Audioslave
'I Dare You', The xx
'Heaven', Depeche Mode
'If You Ever Did Believe', Stevie Nicks
'Get Ur Freak On', Missy Elliott
'Heroes', David Bowie (original)
'Iridescent', Linkin Park
'More', Sisters of Mercy
'Gimme More', Britney Spears
'Try Again', Aaliyah
'The Valley', Emma Ruth Rundle & Thou
'You Gotta Be', Des'ree
'Everybody Here Wants You', Jeff Buckley
'Infra-Red', Placebo
'Sweet Soul Sister', The Cult
'Raingurl', Yaeji
'Heroes', Depeche Mode
'Giant', YUQI
'The Wild Ones', Suede
'Feeling Good', Nina Simone

References

1. Australian Bureau of Statistics. 'Media Release - 2016 Census: Multicultural.' Abs.gov.au, Australian Bureau of Statistics, 27 June 2017, www.abs.gov.au/ausstats/abs@.nsf/lookup/Media%20Release3
2. Strategic White Womanhood, coined by Ruby Hamad and covered in her book, *White Tears/Brown Scars*
3. www.coco-net.org
4. https://adhdjesse.com/posts/omnipotential-the-latent-gift-of-adhd

Acknowledgements

To Ma and Dad for their love, affection, acceptance, support, belief and encouragement throughout my life. Thank you for giving me life and for providing me with strong values, generosity, kindness and freedom to express myself, enabling me to grow and experience life as I choose. I love you both so much.

To Ryan, my partner and husband. Words just aren't enough for how you've positively affected my life. Thank you for being the kind of man who always lifts me up, for always encouraging me, for all the love, for the pep talks and wake-up calls that allowed me to persevere and try different things especially when I didn't believe in myself. I didn't know what love could be until I met you.

To Sahra, my daughter. Becoming Gutsy happened because you came into existence. Nurturing you and watching you grow up has been the biggest privilege of this life. I cannot wait to see what you become in your life, and I hope you will always remember that I am forever in your corner cheering you on and loving you.

To Tash, my BFF. Thank you for always showing up and being the embodiment of what a soul sister is. This book is for us. Thank you for your wisdom, encouragement, laughter, unparalleled big-hearted kindness and sisterhood.

To my parents-in-law, Judith and Rob. I won the in-law lottery with you both. You've both been a constant source of inspiration and motivation backed by strong family values, love and kindness. I love you both.

To Natasha Gilmour, the kind press team, Julie Parker and Beautiful You Coaching Academy, thank you for choosing me as the recipient of The Spirit Scholarship, for all your enthusiasm, encouragement, patience, hard work and support so that I could have my biggest dream realised; a published author!

Thank you again to Julie Parker and the team at Beautiful Coaching Academy for the life coaching training I received in 2018 which inspired me to create a body of work that I'm proud of.

Special thanks to my friends Tash (again), Katherine Mackenzie-Smith, Kris Emery, Naomi Arnold and Angela Morris for your suggestions, thoughts and inputs on my book as I wrote. Your contributions have been invaluable, and I am so grateful. Especially to you Kris for all your book editing wisdom!

Thank you Naomi Arnold (again) and Cameron Airen, co-founders of Feminist Coach Academy for inviting me to be involved in your important work. Thank you to the Advisory Board members, faculty and students for your hard work, expertise, involvement and participation. As a facilitator, I have learned a lot from each of you.

Special mention to friends near and far, Leon Wild, Anuradha Kowtha, Angela Morris, Nailah King, Nadine Chemali and Naomi Hutchings, your friendship, support, kind words of encouragement and help over the years have been lifelines to me to keep going. I value your humour, skills, experience, recommendations, communication and all that each of you are to me.

Special thanks go to my craniosacral work and remedial therapist Ann Apolloni for taking care of my body and spirit over the past six years and for the wonderful friendship that we've developed. Thank you.

Special thanks to my long-time clients Kellie Guenther and Clare Foale. You are both so gifted in what you do and your presence in my life and work continues to inspire me.

Thank you to my clients and students who've completed courses, coaching and programs with me. It means a lot that you chose to work with me to make Gutsy Leadership Circle, Unpack Your Privilege, Be

An Inclusive Coach and Witchuition a part of your life and business.

Thank you to my coaches over these past important years of growth, healing and transformation, Staci Jordan Shelton, Jade McKenzie and Sora Schilling.

Thank you to all the speakers who participated in the Formidable Voices events, LJ Sparrey, Anna Stassen, Jade McKenzie, Sonali Fiske, Sora Schilling, Yolanda Finette, Staci Jordan Shelton, Lena West, McKensie Mack, Ruby Hamad, Kundan Chhabra, Nisha Moodley, Asha Frost, Jolinda Johnson, Mētztli Alexandria, Courtney Napier, Anuradha Kowtha, Tiffany Wong, Rebekah Borucki, Michelle Nicole, Mikaela Egan, Navi Gill and Karen Larbi.

Thank you to the patrons and supporters in my Patreon and ko-fi communities for their contribution and support of my work and writing since 2017. I appreciate and value you all so much for all that you are and do.

About the author

Sharyn Holmes (she/they) is an award-winning leadership and inclusion coach, writer, speaker, artist, creator of the Unpack Your Privilege® anti-oppression framework, Witchuition® leadership circle and Formidable Voices events. Their writing and work dives deep into social justice, spirituality and personal sovereignty. Sharyn leads transformative coaching circles which guides others to bring sacred activism, inclusion and conscious leadership to the heart of their lives and businesses. Sharyn lives in Brisbane, QLD on Turrbal land with their husband, daughter and Italian greyhound pack.

Ingram Content Group UK Ltd.
Milton Keynes UK
UKHW010629220523
422140UK00001B/81